Whitehall Paper 93

Security in Northern Europe: Deterrence, Defence and Dialogue

John Andreas Olsen

LONDON AND NEW YORK

Royal United Services Institute for Defence and Security Studies

Security in Northern Europe: Deterrence, Defence and Dialogue

Whitehall Papers series

First published 2018 on behalf of the Royal United Services Institute for Defence and Security Studies by Routledge Journals,

Published 2019 by Routledge
2 Park Square, Milton Park, Abingdon, Oxon OX14 4RN
52 Vanderbilt Avenue, New York, NY 10017

Routledge is an imprint of the Taylor & Francis Group, an informa business

Series Editor: Professor Malcolm Chalmers
Editor: Emma De Angelis

RUSI is a Registered Charity (No. 210639)
ISBN 13: 978-0-367-10976-9 (pbk)

Cover Image: KNM F314, *Thor Heyerdahl,* followed by KNM F311 *Roald Amundsen,* attending DV-day near Namsos, Norway, during Exercise *Cold Response 2016. Courtesy of Julie Kristiansen Johansen, Norwegian Armed Forces*

Contents

About the Editor

John Andreas Olsen is a colonel in the Royal Norwegian Air Force, currently assigned to London as defence attaché. He is also a visiting professor at the Swedish Defence University and a non-resident senior fellow of the Mitchell Institute for Aerospace Studies. His previous assignments include tours as director of security analyses in the Norwegian Ministry of Defence, deputy commander at NATO Headquarters at Sarajevo, dean of the Norwegian Defence University College and head of the college's division for strategic studies. Olsen is a graduate of the German Command and Staff College and has served as liaison officer to the German Operational Command and as military assistant to the Norwegian Embassy in Berlin. He has a doctorate from De Montfort University and a master's degree from the University of Warwick. Olsen has published several books, including: *Strategic Air Power in Desert Storm* (2003); *John Warden and the Renaissance of American Air Power* (2007); *A History of Air Warfare* (2010); *The Evolution of Operational Art* (2011); *Global Air Power* (2011); *The Practice of Strategy* (2012); *Air Commanders* (2012); *Destination NATO* (2013); *European Air Power* (2014); *Airpower Reborn* (2015); *NATO and the North Atlantic* (2017); *Airpower Applied* (2017); and *Routledge Handbook of Air Power* (2018).

About the Authors

Svein Efjestad became Policy Director at the Norwegian Ministry of Defence (MoD) in 2013. He joined the MoD in 1981 after having completed his master's degree in political science from the University of Oslo and a brief period at the Norwegian Institute of International Relations (NUPI). Efjestad has held different positions in the MoD and served at the Norwegian delegation to NATO from 1986 to 1990. From 1995 to 2013 he served as director general for security policy at the MoD in a number of national and international committees dealing with different security policy issues. In his current position, Efjestad is primarily engaged in policy planning, support to security policy research, the Nordic Defence Cooperation and bilateral defence and security issues. He is also the chairman of the Norwegian Coast Guard Council.

James G Foggo is Commander, Allied Joint Force Command in Naples, Italy. Admiral Foggo is a 1981 graduate of the US Naval Academy, an Olmsted and Moreau Scholar, with a master's degree from Harvard University and a Diplôme d'études approfondies from the University of Strasbourg. Foggo has held several commands, including USS *Oklahoma City* (SSN 723), Submarine Squadron 6, Submarine Group 8, J3 for NATO Joint Task Forces *Odyssey Dawn* and *Unified Protector*, US Sixth Fleet, and NATO Naval Striking and Support Forces. He has directly served the Chairman of the Joint Chiefs of Staff, the Supreme Allied Commander Europe (SACEUR) and was Director of the Navy Staff. He has been awarded the Chevalier de l'Ordre National du Mérite by the French government for his role in improving Franco-American relations and is a member of the Council on Foreign Relations.

Alarik Fritz is a Senior Research Scientist at the Center for Naval Analyses (CNA), a federally funded research and development centre for the US Navy. He joined CNA in 1999 and has managed and conducted a wide variety of analyses while embedded with US Navy and US Marine Corps commands and staffs. His most recent operational tour was as CNA's representative to the US Sixth Fleet in Naples, Italy. Previous tours were with USMC forces during Operations *Enduring Freedom* and *Iraqi Freedom*, and with the US Navy at Fleet Forces Command and Fifth Fleet. He has studied, worked and travelled extensively in Japan, China, Sub-Saharan Africa, South Asia,

Iran, Iraq, Pakistan and other locations in Europe and the Arabian Gulf. He received his PhD from Georgetown University, where his research focused on alliances and coalitions. He received his master's from George Washington University, and his bachelor's from the University of Arizona.

Tomas Jermalavičius is from Lithuania and joined the International Centre for Defence and Security (ICDS) in Tallinn, Estonia in 2008 as a research fellow and, since 2016, has been its head of studies. At ICDS, his research has focused on defence policy and strategy, defence innovation and national resilience. Prior to joining ICDS, he worked at the Baltic Defence College, first as deputy director of the College's Institute of Defence Studies from 2001 to 2004, and later as dean of the college from 2005 to 2008. From 1998–2001 and in 2005, he worked at the Defence Policy and Planning Department of the Lithuanian Ministry of National Defence. In late 1998 and early 1999 he was a visiting fellow at the Swedish National Defence Establishment. Jermalavičius holds a bachelor's degree in political science from the University of Vilnius, a master's in war studies from King's College London and an MBA degree from the University of Liverpool.

Karl-Heinz Kamp is the President of the German Federal Academy for Security Policy (BAKS) in Berlin. He served at the German Council of Foreign Affairs (DGAP), at the Konrad Adenauer Foundation in Berlin and was on a temporary assignment with the Planning Staff of the German Ministry of Foreign Affairs. Between 2007 and 2013 he was the Research Director of the NATO Defense College (NDC) in Rome. In 2009, Secretary Madeleine Albright selected him as one of the advisers for the NATO Expert Group on the New Strategic Concept. In November 2013, he took over the newly created position as Academic Director of the BAKS and in 2015 the German Defence Minister appointed him as its president. Kamp has published about 380 articles on security policy issues in books and journals – including *Foreign Policy*, *Survival*, *Frankfurter Allgemeine Zeitung*, the *Wall Street Journal* and the *Washington Quarterly*.

Eerik Marmei is from Estonia and joined the International Centre for Defence and Security (ICDS) on 1 September 2017. He has a history degree from the University of Tartu and a master's in Peace Studies from the University of Notre Dame (USA). He joined the Estonian Ministry of Foreign Affairs (MFA) in 1993, where he held various positions, including at the permanent representation of Estonia to NATO and at the Estonian embassies in Washington, DC and London. From 2008 to 2010, he was the director of the NATO and EU Department at the Estonian Ministry of Defence and from 2010 to 2013 he was the director of the Security Policy Division at the MFA. He represented Estonia as an ambassador to Poland and Romania from 2013 to 2014 and later was the Estonian ambassador to the United States and Mexico from 2014 to 2017. At ICDS, he specialises in US foreign and security policy, NATO and transatlantic relations.

Magnus Nordenman is the Director of the Transatlantic Security Initiative and the Deputy Director of the Brent Scowcroft Center on International Security at the Atlantic Council. He leads and develops programming and research related to the future of NATO, security in Northern Europe, NATO in the maritime domain and defence and deterrence in the twenty-first century. Before joining the Atlantic Council, Magnus served as a defence analyst with a Washington-based advisory firm, and as a consultant to the defence industry. His insights and commentary have been featured by, among others, the *New York Times*, *Foreign Policy*, *Defense News*, the *BBC*, *CNN*, and *MSNBC*. He is currently working on a book on security in the North Atlantic in the twenty-first century, to be published by the US Naval Institute.

Frans Osinga is an Air Commodore in the Royal Netherlands Air Force, Professor of war studies, Head of the Military Operational Art and Science Section, and Chair of the War Studies Programme at the Netherlands Defence Academy. He teaches courses on coercive diplomacy, contemporary warfare and strategy, and peace operations in the BA War Studies programme and the MA Strategic Studies programme. He is an F-16 pilot, a graduate of the Netherlands Advanced Staff Course and has studied at the USAF Air University. His positions include a tour as the Ministry of Defence Research Fellow at the Clingendael Institute. He wrote his PhD dissertation on the strategic thought of John Boyd at Leiden University. He is the author of more than 60 articles and co-edited books, including: *Military Adaptation in Afghanistan; Targeting: The Challenges of Modern Warfare;* and *Winning Without Killing*.

David Perry is the Vice President, Senior Analyst and a Fellow with the Canadian Global Affairs Institute. He is the author of multiple publications related to defence budgeting, transformation and procurement; published with the Canadian Global Affairs Institute, Conference of Defence Associations Institute, *Defence Studies, Comparative Strategy, International Journal*, and *Journal of Military and Strategic Studies* and is a columnist for the *Canadian Naval Review*. He received his PhD in political science from Carleton University, where his dissertation examined the link between defence budgeting and defence procurement. He is an adjunct professor at the Centre for Military and Strategic Studies at the University of Calgary and a research fellow of the Centre for the Study of Security and Development at Dalhousie University. He was previously the Senior Security and Defence Analyst of the Conference of Defence

Associations Institute and Deputy Director of Dalhousie University's Centre for Foreign Policy Studies.

Peter Roberts is Director of Military Sciences at the Royal United Services Institute, having been the Senior Research Fellow for Sea Power and C4ISR since 2014. He researches and publishes on a range of subjects, including strategy and philosophy, contemporary war, military doctrine and thinking, command and control, naval warfare, ISR, professional military education and disruptive warfare techniques. Roberts was a career Warfare Officer in the Royal Navy, serving as both a Commanding Officer, National Military Representative and in a variety of roles with all three branches of the British armed forces, the US Coast Guard, US Navy, US Marine Corps and intelligence services from a variety of other countries. Roberts has a master's degree in Defence Studies and a doctorate in politics and modern history. He is a Visiting Professor of Modern War at the French Military Academy.

Rolf Tamnes is professor at the Norwegian Institute for Defence Studies (IFS). He served as its director for sixteen years (1996–2012), as head of the international research programme 'Geopolitics in the High North' (2008–2012) and as adjunct professor at the University of Oslo (1995–2009). Tamnes has been a visiting fellow at the Center for Strategic and International Studies (2005–06) and St Antony's College, Oxford (2014). He has also been a public policy scholar at the Woodrow Wilson International Center. Most recently, he chaired the Expert Commission on Norwegian Security and Defence Policy, appointed by the Norwegian MoD, and served as core member in the Afghanistan Inquiry Committee, appointed by the Norwegian government. He has published many books, including co-authored works such as *Common or Divided Security? German and Norwegian Perspectives on Euro-Atlantic Security* (2014) and *Geopolitics and Security in the Arctic: Regional Dynamics in a Global World* (2014).

Alexander 'Sandy' Vershbow is a distinguished fellow at the Brent Scowcroft Center on International Security at the Atlantic Council. Ambassador Vershbow was the deputy secretary general of NATO from February 2012 to October 2016. Prior to his post at NATO, Ambassador Vershbow served for three years as the US assistant secretary of defense for international security affairs. In that position, he was responsible for coordinating US security and defence policies relating to the countries and international organisations of Europe (including NATO), the Middle East and Africa. From 1977 to 2008, Vershbow was a career member of the United States Foreign Service. He served as US ambassador to NATO (1998–2001); to the Russian Federation (2001–05); and to the Republic of Korea (2005–08).

Marcin Zaborowski is a Lecturer at Łazarski University, Warsaw, Poland and the former director of the Polish Institute of International Relations (PISM) (2010–15). Under his leadership, PISM was named in the ranking by UN University as the most influential think tank in Central and Eastern Europe and the most influential in the world with a budget under $5 million. In his past capacity, Zaborowski served at the EU Institute for Security Studies in Paris, where he ran the transatlantic programme. He gained his master's and PhD at the University of Birmingham and is the author of numerous publications including *Germany, Poland and Europe* (2003), *Polish Foreign and Security Priorities* (2007) and *Bush's Legacy and America's Next Foreign Policy* (2008).

Preface

Security in Northern Europe is a follow-on to *NATO and the North Atlantic: Revitalising Collective Defence*, published in March 2017 as a RUSI Whitehall Paper. While the previous paper explored the renewed importance of the North Atlantic Ocean from the perspectives of the US, the UK and Norway in particular, this new study takes a broader approach by including the views of all members of Europe's Northern Group, adjunct waters and countries in North America.

Although the new security landscape is multi-faceted and complex, the resurgence of state-based aggression represents the dominant factor. With NATO's Article 5 commitments now back at the forefront of the Alliance's mission, certain regions, which until recently attracted little attention from Western states, have regained strategic relevance. One of the most important is Northern Europe. This Whitehall Paper identifies both individual and common challenges and suggests effective national and collective reactions. While the individual chapters can stand alone, they also complement and build on each other to construct a cohesive analysis. This, in turn, can help NATO members and key partners to offer a stronger response on the basis of better information regarding each country's priorities, attitudes and institutional affiliations.

The authors bring unique insight and knowledge to their geographically oriented case studies. They have worked on defence and security in various capacities and areas of responsibility and can account for the interplay among historical, cultural, economic, social and political factors that define a state. While their views carry authoritative weight, the opinions and conclusions in this volume are those of the authors and the editor; they do not represent the official position of any government or institution; indeed, scholarly independence has been encouraged.

I am grateful to the authors for their contributions both to this volume and to an extensive outreach programme, which, like the previous study, includes conferences in several countries to encourage an informed debate. I am much obliged to Dr Robin Allers and Colonel Per Erik Solli who provided insightful critiques on the evolving manuscript, and am again in debt to Margaret S MacDonald for excellent editorial counsel. I am also thankful to RUSI and especially the Publications Editor, Dr Emma De Angelis, for first-rate cooperation from concept to publication.

John Andreas Olsen
August 2018

FOREWORD

STUART PEACH

Russia's illegal annexation of Crimea in February 2014 and its continued sponsorship of separatist activity in eastern Ukraine served as a wake-up call for Europe. It was the strategic surprise that we could have foreseen. The invasion of Georgia and the start of the Russian military modernisation programme in 2008, combined with Russia's increasingly belligerent rhetoric and higher risk appetite, had already started to challenge the Western way of life, underpinned by our fundamental values and principles. Since then, Russia has improved its military capabilities considerably and conducted a series of offensively oriented large-scale exercises. It has expanded its military infrastructure in the Arctic and Russian submarines are undertaking aggressive patrols near Atlantic cables as part of the country's broader interest in unconventional methods of warfare. Russia is also increasingly active in the Baltic Sea, at times breaching airspace sovereignty, and once again the waters of the North Atlantic have become a contested area. In sum, NATO members and partners are now facing a step-change in military aggression from Russia across several fronts.

As Vice Chief and later Chief of the UK Defence Staff from 2013 to 2018, I witnessed first-hand how NATO's political leaders and military commanders rose to the occasion and stood together to strengthen the Alliance's primary mission of deterrence and collective defence. The NATO summits in Wales (2014) and Warsaw (2016) not only brought NATO 'back to Europe', but also initiated closer cooperation with NATO's two most important non-aligned partners, Finland and Sweden. NATO is enhancing its forward presence in the eastern part of the Alliance, with four multinational battlegroups deployed in Estonia, Latvia, Lithuania and Poland on a rotational basis. These battlegroups, led by the UK, Canada, Germany and the US respectively, are multinational and combat-ready, demonstrating the strength of the transatlantic bond. The northern

European states have all expanded their defence budgets, and their respective national defence and security reviews are more ambitious and committed than they have been for decades. NATO is also increasingly focusing on the need to maintain free access through the North Atlantic and is updating and exercising contingency plans. In essence, NATO is refocusing its efforts to become better prepared to deal with a resurgent Russia.

At least three challenges are likely to preoccupy the countries of northern Europe. The first concerns NATO's ability, as an organisation and institution, to serve as the overarching framework for European security and deliver collective security to our people. The recent agreement to reform NATO's command structure will strengthen the organisation's regional profile. It is a positive development that Sweden and Finland have achieved preferential status in NATO plans. Increased EU–NATO cooperation can produce a better division of labour and should include satisfactory agreements to ensure the integration of Norway, Iceland and the UK into future European security structures. Complementing NATO response options, the British-led Joint Expeditionary Force provides a pool of flexible high-readiness forces and cross-governmental departments that can be tailored to meet any emergency, from humanitarian assistance to combat operations. Frameworks such as Nordic Defence Cooperation and the Northern Group are useful for strengthening the region. Yet, as an alliance of 29 vastly different states, NATO needs to balance its efforts on two counts: increasing regional bilateral, trilateral and multinational cooperation must strengthen, not be at the expense of, NATO cohesion and solidarity; and deterrence and defence must go hand in hand with dialogue and active engagement to improve relations with Russia.

A second challenge lies in maintaining solid transatlantic relations. In military terms, NATO must ensure sea control to keep sea lines of communications open. The US and Canada remain crucial for the region's security, including for non-aligned Sweden and Finland. With the European Deterrence Initiative, Washington has proved its commitment to the region and the US Congress serves as a guarantor of that commitment. As NATO reforms a new command in Norfolk, Virginia, with a dedicated focus on the North Atlantic, this will further strengthen the all-important transatlantic link. At the same time, the prospect of changes in the US's commitment – whether because of shifting priorities such as the rebalancing towards Asia or because of frustration over seemingly insufficient European contributions to transatlantic burden sharing – presents a major concern to regional actors and should drive closer regional cooperation. Increased European defence budgets are likely to facilitate stronger US and Canadian commitments in the future.

Strengthening the Northern European portion of the Western security community is an important part of the overall strategy.

A third challenge relates to the wider security architecture. Northern Europe consists of countries that have a strong tradition of taking part in out-of-area stabilisation operations under a UN or coalition mandate. Football teams cannot defend only on the goal line, and Northern European countries have made notable contributions to international security efforts where and when needed, whether by participating in military operations in the Balkans, Afghanistan, the Middle East and Africa, assisting victims of the refugee crisis in the Mediterranean, or responding to catastrophes caused by nature rather than man. As states strengthen defence at home, they must continue to contribute to security abroad. The only way to deal with terrorism in its various manifestations is through unity of effort and the collective will to respond upstream.

The Northern Group countries have a unique relationship with each other and are in an ideal position to respond to the new risks and opportunities that we all face. The way we meet new challenges will determine the future security landscape in the North. We must all think anew, be more creative and adapt to the new situation. We must not adhere to old norms for sentimental or nostalgic reasons, but instead incorporate modern deterrence into our defence plans and continue to reinvent ourselves in order to maximise peace and prosperity in accordance with the core values of democracy, individual liberty and the rule of law.

Security in Northern Europe offers fresh, balanced and sophisticated insights from experts in the field. The case studies will help inform political and military plans and documents and contribute to a productive public debate over the direction of defence. Importantly, the authors consider the concept of security as a whole before examining its individual components. I am very pleased with this Whitehall Paper's comprehensive approach to security. I recommend it to both civilian policymakers and the military.

Air Chief Marshal Sir Stuart Peach GBE KCB ADC DL
Chairman of the NATO Military Committee

INTRODUCTION
SECURITY IN NORTHERN EUROPE

JOHN ANDREAS OLSEN

Challenge

A state's prioritisation of defence waxes and wanes according to threat assessments. Currently, defence issues have regained an urgency that Europe has not witnessed for at least three decades. Russia's aggressive rhetoric and behaviour, significant numbers of forces on high readiness, revitalisation of sea control and sea denial in its northern bastion, reinvestment in forces and dual-use infrastructure along its Arctic coast, and ambitious military modernisation programme with emphasis on long-range precision weapons present a major concern for all of Europe, and for the eastern and northern countries in particular. Heightened submarine activity in the North Atlantic challenges open sea lines of communication between North America and Europe and the ability to provide transatlantic reinforcement in a potential conflict. Russia's offensive and at times aggressive manoeuvre exercises that include simulated attacks in the Nordic-Baltic countries increase tension still further. Moscow has also engaged in active cyber attacks and has demonstrated innovative hybrid strategies. A recent US study identifies four capability areas of major concern: long-range precision strike; integrated air and missile defence; cyber and electronic warfare; and, not least, nuclear forces.[1] *FOCUS 2018* – the Norwegian Intelligence Service's annual assessment of the current security challenge – concludes that Russia has 'modernised and trained its armed forces to a standard that expands the Kremlin's scope for action, including in the High North and

[1] Heather A Conley, Jeffrey Rathke and Matthew Melino, *Enhanced Deterrence in the North: A 21st Century European Engagement Strategy* (Washington, DC: Center for Strategic and International Studies, February 2018).

the Arctic'.[2] NATO views the Russian challenge in terms of not only growing capabilities and expanding exercises, but also of Moscow's willingness to employ military force to achieve political ends.[3] The invasions of Georgia and Ukraine demonstrate that Russia is prepared to violate international law to advance its national interests and regional ambitions. The Kremlin seems determined to undermine the European security order and weaken the transatlantic link. In sum, Russia's military build-up and subversive activities constitute today's most important challenge to the defence of Europe.

Focus

With NATO returning its focus to its core mission of deterrence and collective defence, certain regions have regained strategic prominence. One of the most important is Northern Europe, here defined as the twelve countries that constitute 'The Northern Group'.[4] This Whitehall Paper examines various national concerns and challenges and recommends actions to ensure that the region remains prosperous and safe. It offers geostrategic insight into the northern members of NATO, with the goal of helping national decision-makers compare and contrast defence arrangements to find better solutions to deal with the transformed security realities for Northern Europe.

The challenges posed by Russia have sharpened NATO's focus and strengthened its sense of purpose, but the diversity and distinctions among allies and partners are significant. The key actors in each part of Northern Europe have different security priorities, with Sweden, Finland, the Baltic States, Poland and Germany being primarily 'Baltic Sea oriented', while the United Kingdom, the Netherlands and Norway naturally take a greater interest in the North Atlantic region. Denmark, due to its sovereignty over Greenland, has a foot in both camps. The US and Canada are strongly committed to security in Europe, because of both geography and historical-cultural-societal ties, but need to balance concerns in the Atlantic and the Pacific. One of the premises underlying

---

2 Norwegian Intelligence Service, 'FOCUS 2018: The Norwegian Intelligence Service's Assessment of Current Security Challenges', 2018.

3 NATO, 'Brussels Summit Declaration', press release, 11 July 2018, para. 2, <https://www.nato.int/cps/en/natohq/official_texts_156624.htm>, accessed 23 July 2018.

4 The Northern Group is a forum in which members come together informally to discuss defence and security issues common to Northern European nations and to explore new opportunities for working together. The membership consists of Denmark, Estonia, Finland, Germany, Iceland, Latvia, Lithuania, the Netherlands, Norway, Poland, Sweden and the UK.

this Whitehall Paper is that to master the new security reality, the Northern Group countries must not only comprehend Russia, but also understand themselves and acknowledge the importance of closer cooperation. Although it focuses on existing regional arrangements for defence cooperation, the paper underscores the vital importance of preserving the transatlantic link in today's increasingly complex and multifaceted security environment.

Structure

Security in Northern Europe is divided into three sections. The opening section contains essays on three geographic areas. The chapter on the High North – which emphasises the maritime domain that stretches from the Baltic Sea to the North Atlantic and the Barents Sea and serves as a scene-setter for the entire book – is followed by chapters on the Baltic and Nordic regions respectively. The eight countries comprising these regions share a common geostrategic outlook, although the details vary considerably. For example, each of the Baltic states has unique internal political and societal contexts, strategic cultures and national defence models, but as a group they display only minor differences in their threat perceptions and their call for NATO to assist in managing Russia.

The second section offers country-specific case studies of the 'big four' economic powers in the Northern Group constellation: the UK, the Netherlands, Germany and Poland. These four countries have a special affiliation with the Nordic-Baltic region, as they have traditionally looked north and east to ensure their own security. They are linked by strong economic bonds and also seek mechanisms for enhanced defence cooperation and coordination. Still, their national agendas dictate different priorities. For example, the UK has a special responsibility to secure freedom of manoeuvre in its 'northern backyard', while Poland is yet again a front line state in a potential conflict.

Acknowledging the geostrategic significance of the transatlantic link, the third section of the book includes chapters on the United States and Canada, ending with some reflections from a NATO perspective. The defence of Northern Europe, spanning NATO members and key partners, depends on the Alliance's ability to execute its core mission of deterrence and collective defence, and a credible NATO depends principally on US leadership.

Consequently, attempting to deal with defence and security in Northern Europe without the US makes no sense. As for Canada, its contribution to NATO's Enhanced Forward Presence in Latvia and recent white paper on defence highlight that country's renewed commitment to Europe in times of ambiguity.

Thesis

The paper presents a three-fold thesis. First, credible deterrence and collective defence depend on the Alliance's cohesion and ability to devise a broad-based response to Russia: one that is unified and theatre-wide, treating Northern Europe as a single entity, encompassing the maritime domain that connects the Baltic Sea with the North Atlantic. This includes the full spectrum of response options, from high-end capabilities and rapid readiness to move to total defence concepts such as border-crossing procedures, whole-of-government approaches and industry–defence cooperation.

Second, and equally important, NATO as a whole and Northern Europe specifically must ensure that the transatlantic link is not merely preserved, but strengthened in the current political climate. Europe and North America depend on each other for prosperity and security. While the European states must increase their defence budgets, the US remains the single most important actor in any strategy to contest and contain Russia. All NATO countries bordering Russia see the US as their strongest and most important ally.

Third, to ensure a secure and safe Europe, NATO members, together with Sweden and Finland, must both strengthen deterrence and defence initiatives and constantly seek dialogue and engagement with Russia. NATO should enter this dialogue from a position of strength and never forget Winston Churchill's dictum that 'jaw-jaw is better than war-war'. This book's key message is that this two-fold track of deterrence and defence combined with dialogue and engagement can only achieve its goals if all parties involved have a profound understanding of each countries' specifics and communalities.

This Whitehall Paper seeks to elaborate on a recipe for peace, security and stability in the whole of the Euro-Atlantic area: mastering the challenges of the current security environment demands a unified approach, in which Northern European countries strengthen cooperation among themselves and reinforce the transatlantic bond to enhance deterrence and collective defence, while at the same time seeking to build a peaceful, mutually satisfactory and constructive relationship with Russia.

I. THE HIGH NORTH: A CALL FOR A COMPETITIVE STRATEGY

ROLF TAMNES

Russia's military build-up and subversive activities constitute the most important challenge to the defence of Europe. Russia has revitalised its so-called 'bastion' concept,[1] which includes sea control of northern waters, sea denial down into the Greenland–Iceland–UK (GIUK) gap, and force projection into the North Atlantic to disrupt trade flows and military freedom of manoeuvre. More broadly, from the Arctic to the Mediterranean, an arc of steel – built on precision-guided missiles that can be launched from the sea-, air- and land-based platforms – is descending across Europe. US military reinforcements to Europe depend on open transatlantic sea lines of communication, and Russia's bastion defence and anti-access capabilities put the freedom of the transatlantic sea lanes to the test.

Since 2014, NATO has taken significant steps to build a more credible deterrent and defence against Russia's build-up and increasingly provocative actions, especially by establishing an enhanced forward presence on its eastern flank. It has also embarked on a venture to strengthen the defence of the northern flank and the North Atlantic. Importantly, it is revamping its command structure. These are significant steps that demonstrate adaptability and unity, but NATO needs to do far more.

This chapter focuses on the expansion of Russia's military capabilities in the High North and its implications for Western security. It highlights the asymmetric relationship between Russia and Norway and emphasises the need for early military assistance from key allies in the event of a conflict

---

[1] The bastion defence combines a layered defence of attack and multipurpose submarines, underwater sensors, surface combatants, ground-based systems with a great variety of weapons, and air power.

to ensure smooth and integrated escalation for response. It also reflects on Iceland's geostrategic role and the need to boost NATO's maritime posture significantly to prevent Russian forces from cutting the all-important transatlantic sea lines of communication. The chapter's main messages are that the High North is central to a Europe 'free, whole and at peace', and that NATO should formulate a competitive strategy, taking advantage of its own strengths and of Russia's weaknesses.

Geography and History

The circumpolar Arctic is an ocean surrounded by three continents and five littoral states. The region represents an example of successful cooperation and innovative government in non-military spheres.[2] The economic and strategic importance of the Arctic will likely increase significantly in the longer run. Climate change and rapid ice melt are opening up Arctic waterways – including a new passage to Asia – and boosting the exploitation of the region's extensive resources. A more powerful Asia, and China in particular, will play a prominent role also in the Arctic and contribute to making it a more central part of global geopolitics.[3]

This chapter pays particular attention to the European High North, comprising the northern parts of the Nordic countries and Russia, with Norway and Russia as the core, and including the oceans and islands in the Barents and Norwegian seas from Novaya Zemlya to Iceland. In strategic terms, the region is largely defined by the reach of Russian military power based on the Kola Peninsula. The High North is an essential part of the North Atlantic strategic geometry: protection of sea lanes relies on the ability to contain Russia in this area and on bases in the Northern Triangle – notably in Norway, Iceland and the UK.

The High North came to the forefront of NATO concerns in the 1970s. The accelerated build-up of the Soviet Northern Fleet underscored the asymmetry of the relationship between Norway and the Soviet Union, and bolstered Norway's efforts to tie NATO more closely to the defence of the north. In 1973 there was a turning point as Russian strategic submarines (SSBNs) began to receive intercontinental-range missiles which could

[2] Michael Byers, 'Crises and International Cooperation: An Arctic Case Study', *International Relations* (Vol. 31, No. 4, 2017); Andreas Østhagen, 'High North, Low Politics: Maritime Cooperation with Russia in the Arctic', *Arctic Review on Law and Politics* (Vol. 7, No. 1, 2016).

[3] Rolf Tamnes and Kristine Offerdal (eds), *Geopolitics and Security in the Arctic: Regional Dynamics in a Global World* (London and New York, NY: Routledge Global Security Studies, 2014), pp. 167–77; Pavel Devyatkin, 'Russia's Arctic Strategy', Parts I–IV, Arctic Institute, February 2018, https://www.thearcticinstitute.org/experts/pavel-devyatkin/, accessed 15 April 2018.

target the US from the Arctic Ocean and the Sea of Okhotsk, referred to as 'sanctuaries' and 'bastions'.[4] The main mission of the Northern Fleet's general-purpose capability was now to protect and ensure the survival of Soviet SSBNs and their supporting infrastructure. The shift raised the spectre of a *Mare Sovieticum* in the northern waters and brought the north closer to the geopolitical centre of the Cold War.[5] There was some truth to the dictum that 'a war might be won in the Fulda Gap but it might be lost at the GIUK gap'.[6]

Initially, NATO's defence of the north and its maritime domain came to rely heavily on bases in the Northern Triangle. From 1974 on, Norway was included in the US Air Force (USAF) Co-located Operating Bases programme. In 1981, the US Marine Corps assigned an amphibious brigade to the defence of Norway and combined this with the pre-positioning of the brigade's heavy equipment in caves in mid-Norway. Britain, the Netherlands, Germany, and Canada also increased their commitments in the High North. In the second phase, beginning in the early 1980s, the US and NATO launched their forward maritime strategies. By putting more pressure on Soviet naval forces, notably strategic submarines, they hoped to reduce the threat to the Atlantic sea lanes and secure the routes for reinforcements to Europe.[7]

The main role of the Norwegian armed forces in the event of war would be to delay and hold a Soviet offensive in the north until effective assistance arrived from abroad. More broadly, Norway could contribute significantly to the common cause by assigning a main portion of its large merchant fleet to the NATO effort to ferry supplies from North America to Europe, and by directing its strong intelligence service to monitor Soviet strategic nuclear forces and other activities in northwest Russia.

Iceland constituted another point of the Northern Triangle. The country has no armed forces of its own, so on the basis of the defence agreement of 1951 its security has been guaranteed by the US, which until 2006 maintained a sizeable military force at the Keflavik airbase. Iceland's ambiguous attitude to the US presence led to much anxiety in NATO, whose security depended heavily on Iceland as 'a stepping-stone' and as 'an unsinkable carrier', notably for surveillance and anti-submarine

---

[4] Rolf Tamnes, *The United States and the Cold War in the High North* (Oslo: Ad Notam, 1991), pp. 228–29.

[5] Rolf Tamnes and Sven G Holtsmark, 'The Geopolitics in the Arctic in Historical Perspective', in Tamnes and Offerdal, *Geopolitics and Security in the Arctic*, p. 27.

[6] John Andreas Olsen (ed.), *NATO and the North Atlantic: Revitalising Collective Defence*, RUSI Whitehall Paper 87 (London: RUSI, 2017), p. 4.

[7] Jacob Børresen et al., *Norsk forsvarshistorie, bd. 5, Allianseforsvar i endring, 1970–2000 [The History of Norwegian Defence, Vol. 5, The Changing Character of Alliance Defence 1970–2000]* (Bergen: Eide forlag, 2004), pp. 53–66.

warfare operations in the North Atlantic. In 1956 and 1971, left-wing governments in Reykjavik called for the abrogation or extensive revision of the defence treaty and the removal of US troops from Iceland. In the early 1970s, the government was prepared to use both the US military presence and Iceland's membership in NATO to fight the 'Cod War'. In the end, compromises were found, and Reykjavik remained an important member of the alliance.[8]

The High North in Putin's Military Strategy

The main objectives of President Vladimir Putin's policy are to secure the survival of his regime and restore Russia's great-power status. Since 2008, Russia has invested heavily in the modernisation of its armed forces. It has been a remarkable, if incomplete, success. Russia's methods of exerting influence have become steadily more anomalous, echoing the behaviour of a rogue state and KGB-type subversion. Russia plays the role of a strategic spoiler in conflict-ridden regions, violates fundamental rules and norms of the international order, and uses cyber-capabilities to collect intelligence information, attack infrastructure and manipulate the political and public debate in the West.

Some of these features are apparent also in Russian policies in the High North. Pressure, intimidation and hybrid actions in the grey areas between war and peace provide Russia with options to disrupt Norwegian and NATO decision-making and undermine Western unity. But at the same time, Norway and Russia have a shared interest in working together in areas such as border issues, fishery management and soft-security challenges. In general, governance mechanisms in these fields function well for the north.

Russia's strategy in the north is an integral part of its grand strategy. Russia has restored a capacity for theatre-scale warfare, led by Joint Strategic Commands directly under the General Staff. Its military posture is oriented to achieving rapid peace-to-war transition, seizing the strategic initiative and employing military power to intimidate and coerce. To achieve this, the force posture is optimised for high readiness, prompt mobilisation, and quick movement of large forces over long distances.[9]

Within this framework, Russia's priorities in the north are determined by the region's geostrategic position. The north remains important in

---

8 Valur Ingimundarson, *The Rebellious Ally: Iceland, the United States, and the Politics of Empire 1945–2006* (St Louis and Dordrecht: Republic of Letters Publishing, 2011), pp. 70–3, 99–134.

9 Diego A Ruiz Palmer, *Theatre Operations, High Commands and Large-Scale Exercises in Soviet and Russian Military Practice: Insights and Implications* (Rome: NATO Defense College, Fellowship monograph 12, May 2018).

Russia's nuclear strategy. In 2007 there was a significant increase in strategic bomber flights, with Tu-95MS Bear H and Tu-160 Blackjack aircraft observed over the Arctic and along European coasts, often combined with shorter flights by non-strategic bombers, such as the Tu-22M Backfire and Su-24 Fencer. From 2008 on, after years of decline, Russia has also placed greater emphasis on re-establishing its bastion defence concept, resulting in a higher, sustained level of patrol activity. While Russia describes this as a defensive measure, it presents severe challenges to the countries affected, partly because of Russia's other more provocative actions.[10]

Russia is building an extensive military and dual-use infrastructure along the entire Arctic rim to support offensive operations, protect Russia from incoming bombers and missiles, and manage soft-security challenges. It is modernising a great number of new airbases and has deployed intermediate- and long-range air-defence systems in the continental portion of the Arctic, from Murmansk to Chukotka, and on many island territories. Airbases in Franz Josef Land and Novaya Zemlya have been prepared for tactical and strategic aircraft to undertake defensive and offensive combat operations. Russia is also spending significant sums to build logistical bases, search-and-rescue centres, and Federal Security Service (FSB) border-guard stations along the Northern Sea Route. To strengthen planning and operations in the Arctic and North Atlantic, Russia established the Arctic Joint Strategic Command in 2014, with the Northern Fleet as its main striking force. This command is the pivot in Russia's anti-access strategy in the maritime domain.[11]

New weapons' systems and technologies contribute to strengthening Russia's strategic force and the defence of submarines. The *Borei-* and *Delta IV*-class strategic submarines, based at Gadzhiyevo on the Kola Peninsula, can carry more than 400 strategic nuclear warheads in total, which constitute around 60 per cent of Russia's sea-based nuclear deterrent.[12]

---

[10] Rolf Tamnes, 'The Significance of the North Atlantic and the Norwegian Contribution', in Olsen (ed.), *NATO and the North Atlantic*, pp. 8–31.

[11] Kristian Åtland, 'The Building up of Russia's Military Potential in the Arctic Region and Possible Elements of its Deterrence', Centre for Russian Studies, 12 June 2017, <http://r-studies.org/cms/index.php?action=news/view_details&news_id=43590&lang=eng>, accessed 15 April 2018; Tamnes, 'The Significance of the North Atlantic and the Norwegian Contribution', p. 27.

[12] Roger N McDermott and Tor Bukkvoll, *Russia in the Precision-Strike Regime – Military Theory, Procurement and Operational Impact*, FFI Report (Kjeller: Norwegian Defence Research Establishment, August 2017); Hans M Kristensen and Robert S Norris, 'Russian Nuclear Forces, 2017', *Bulletin of the Atomic Scientists* (Vol. 73, No. 2, 2017).

Bastion defence has become very robust, mostly due to the high quality of Russia's attack submarines – notably the *Akula II*-class, and the quiet *Severodvinsk*-class multipurpose submarines – armed with advanced cruise missiles as well as torpedoes. They are ably prepared to destroy enemy ships and targets ashore, and pose a manifest threat to the UK's SSBN deterrent.

Given these patterns, the Russian navy has become a new form of dual fleet, consisting of on the one hand a strategic submarine-based deterrent and, on the other, attack submarines and smaller surface ships, especially frigates and corvettes, capable of carrying a large number of torpedoes and cruise missiles and of playing a key role in both anti-access efforts and protecting the strategic force in particular. The new State Armaments Programme 2018–27 will reduce funding for the navy. Although this will limit the building of large surface ships and undercut Russia's aspirations of constructing a blue-water navy, it will not affect the strategic capability and the navy's anti-access capabilities.[13]

Russia's military posture, relying on an improving capacity for theatre-scale warfare, accentuates the asymmetrical character of the relationship with its small Western neighbours. In terms of operations in the north, Russia has the advantage of space, time and power. It also has improved readiness and the ability to transfer considerable land and air reinforcements at short notice. In a worst-case scenario, Russia could seek to impose a fait accompli before allies decide to engage or reinforcements arrive.

The challenge was clearly demonstrated in the 2017 *Zapad* ['West'] exercise, carried out in conjunction with the Northern Fleet's annual joint exercise and an exercise along the Northern Sea Route. The key objective of these exercises in the north was to test the operability of the Arctic Joint Strategic Command. The backbone of any operation in the region consists of the regional manoeuvre forces, notably the 200th Independent Motor-Rifle Brigade, 61st Naval Infantry Brigade and 80th Independent Motor-Rifle Brigade, as well as offensive and defensive Spetsnaz forces. In this exercise, Russia transferred forces and equipment by rail and air from the Western and Central military districts on a scale not seen since the Cold War. The reinforcement operation included both Backfire bombers and advanced missile systems. S-400 anti-aircraft missile systems had already been deployed to the Kola Peninsula in 2014. This time, in 2017, Iskander land-attack missile systems – able to carry missiles with a range of around 500 km – were for the first time moved to the north and deployed close to the Norwegian border, from where they could reach a

---

[13] Dmitry Gorenburg, 'Russia's Military Modernization Plans: 2018–2027', PONARS Eurasia Policy Memo No. 495 (November 2017).

major part of northern Norway. Russia also transferred three battalion tactical groups to Kola, including one from the 98th Guards Airborne Division based at Ivanovo, which is probably assigned the task of reinforcing the Arctic. In addition, Russia carried out extensive electronic warfare operations.[14]

Russia has accompanied the military build-up with more provocative actions. Traditionally, offensive flights and intimidation have been more frequent in the Baltic region than in the north; a simulated bomber attack of March 2008 against military installations in the Bodø area in northern Norway was among the exceptions. In spring 2017, Russia launched three simulated offensives with bomber aircraft: against a Norwegian intelligence station in Vardø; against Exercise *Eastern Atlantic* off northern Norway; and against Bodø during Exercise *Arctic Challenge*.[15] Russia has carried out further simulated missions since. Should this trend continue, it might weaken cooperation in areas that have traditionally been insulated from international tensions.

Managing Russia: Norway's Security Priorities

Developments under Putin have energised Norway to engage its NATO allies more closely in the defence of the north. Since 2014, Norway's armed forces have undergone major readjustment to cope with the resurgent Russia. Norwegian authorities have worked systematically to revitalise NATO collective defence, especially by urging the Alliance to reform its command structure and its posture in the North Atlantic for high-intensity conflict. Norway and NATO are much better prepared in the High North today than they were some years ago, but the shortcomings and the gaps in force ratio are still significant.

Norway's own defence funding is growing. The current long-term plan stipulates an increase of NOK830 million ($980 million), or 16.5 per cent, from 2017 to 2020. While this is a major expansion, the new total is equivalent to only 1.6 per cent of GNP. Without further significant growth in defence funding, the budget will therefore not reach NATO's 2 per cent defence spending pledge by 2024. This could put a major strain on the bilateral relationship with the US, commanded by a president who is blasting NATO allies for not meeting the target.

---

[14] Norwegian Intelligence Service, 'FOCUS 2018: The Norwegian Intelligence Service's Assessment of Current Security Challenges', 2018; Morten Haga Lunde, 'Etterretningssjefens årstale 2018', Oslo Militære Samfund, 5 March 2018, <https://forsvaret.no/etjenesten/etterretningssjefens-aarlige-tale>, accessed 15 April 2018; Igor Sutaygin with Justin Bronk, *Russia's New Ground Forces: Capabilities, Limitations and Implications for International Security*, RUSI Whitehall Paper 89 (London: RUSI, 2017), pp. 122–29.

[15] Lunde, 'Etterretningssjefens årstale 2018'.

Current defence plans have three priorities. First, Norway intends to replace its F-16s with up to 52 F-35 Lightning II combat aircraft, and replace its *Ula*-class submarines with four German *Type 212* boats. Norway's armed forces are hereby set on a changed course, with the balance of military striking power – and the core of Norway's deterrent capacity – shifting to the air and maritime domains. This marks a significant change compared to the Cold War, when Norway relied heavily on the army, whose main mission was to fight defensively in northern Norway until reinforced by allies. Second, Norway plans to improve intelligence and surveillance to keep better watch over Russia's military activities. This relies on considerable US financial and technological support. Third, Norway plans to station more land forces in Finnmark county in the northeast, operating as a 'deterrent by tripwire' to hinder a possible Russian fait accompli.[16]

The ultimate purpose of such a tripwire is to engage the Alliance. While Norway will normally deal on its own with minor incidents and low-intensity crises, it does not have the muscle to defend itself against a major assault, and military help will be crucial from the beginning. Escalation must be as seamless as possible, ensuring that the augmentation of Norwegian forces and allied reinforcement take place in an integrated manner. Norway does not permit the stationing of allied forces in the country during peacetime, and this makes defence more difficult. Notwithstanding this restraint, allied support to deterrence and defence should be credible if:

- Norway and NATO receive strategic or tactical warning and have time to respond.
- Some allied forces are in place *before* actual war breaks out – one of the alternatives might be to use forces from allied countries that are training and exercising in Norway.
- NATO or key allies make a firm decision to engage immediately, forcing Russia to realise that further steps will bring it into war with NATO.
- Allied air- and sea-based missiles are engaged from the outset.
- Substantial allied reinforcements begin to move, signalling to Russia that it will face overwhelming superiority.

While it is important to stand up to Russia, Norway is destined to live alongside it. Since the early Cold War, Norway has therefore pursued a twin-track security policy, combining deterrence and defence with reassurance and dialogue. In order to reassure its neighbour, a series of

---

[16] International Institute for Strategic Studies, *The Military Balance 2018* (London: Routledge 2018), pp. 75–80.

restraints has been imposed on allied peacetime military activity in Norway. They include a ban on nuclear weapons and the stationing of allied forces. Furthermore, to keep the High North an area of relatively low tension, Norway allows only smaller foreign military units to train and exercise in Finnmark county, and normally does not permit operations by foreign military aircraft over the Barents Sea from bases in Norway. Such reassurance goes hand in hand with the goal of seeking cooperation when possible and appropriate. Hence, whereas Norway in 2014 joined EU sanctions and suspended major parts of its bilateral military cooperation with Russia, the two countries continue to work together in areas such as coast guard, border guard activities, and search and rescue. This 'Norwegian model' of combining deterrence and defence with reassurance and dialogue might also be appropriate for other allies.

NATO and US Reorientation

NATO is adapting to a 'new normal', albeit slowly. The first substantial step has consisted of strengthening deterrence on the Alliance's eastern flank. The second has involved the redesign of the NATO Response Force (NRF), in particular the creation of the Very High Readiness Joint Task Force (VJTF), NATO's only rapid-reaction force. The VJTF is a small force, and its deployment depends on collective decision in NATO, so it is not certain that operations in the north will receive high priority. A third step has been the formulation of graduated response plans, including a plan for Norway, the North Atlantic and the North Sea. The fourth step is to strengthen the allied maritime posture and command structure, including a new joint command in the US for the North Atlantic. More broadly, NATO is about to improve preparedness, readiness, speed of decision-making, and unity of command, as well as binding graduated response plans together into a theatre-wide approach.

While all these steps are important from the perspective of the High North, the Alliance cannot set up a solid defence unless it starts thinking in terms of competitive strategy. NATO's current mode of thinking is static, symmetric and predictable, leaving Russia, which plans for theatre-scale operations, the initiative to decide when, where and how to act. A competitive strategy is the art of creating power.[17] This means that NATO should capitalise on the strengths of the Western states, and identify and exploit Russia's weaknesses – while at the same time looking for

---

[17] Andrew Krepinevich and Barry Watts, *The Last Warrior, Andrew Marshall and the Shaping of Modern American Defense Strategy* (New York, NY: Basic Books, 2015), pp. 166–68; Lawrence Freedman, *Strategy, A History* (Oxford: Oxford University Press, 2014), p. xii.

incentives to engage Russia, bearing in mind that ultimately security can be obtained only through cooperative undertakings.

NATO could improve its competitive position in Northern Europe in many ways. The Alliance should use new technology and concepts to offset its disadvantage of space, time and power in the northern region. Equally important is to optimise the potential of theatre-wide strategies and operations, notably across the whole Northern European front line from the Baltic to the High North. Finland and Sweden are about to become functional allies of NATO based on a web of agreements that incrementally prepare them to operate together in a crisis, should their governments decide to do so. Further developing this partnership would also make Russia realise that an isolated assault in the High North is not an option, as it would likely unleash a much broader Western response: Russia would meet a significant combination of combat air capabilities, as illustrated in the biennial *Arctic Challenge* exercise. A NATO campaign on the northern flank would also benefit from logistical support through Sweden and Finland, just as bases and harbours in Norway can support operations on the eastern flank.

Such a combined effort by NATO and partner countries along the whole front line in Northern Europe, connecting the eastern and northern flanks, can contribute to solidifying Western defences and making them a more credible deterrent. To further enhance such a forward-based approach, the Alliance will also have to strengthen the connection between the Northern European front line and the North Atlantic. Western operations in the northern waters and the High North are crucial to success. They must be truly joint in character, but in this theatre of operations amphibious and maritime forces, particularly UK, Dutch and US capabilities, play a prominent and unique role.

The US has articulated a strong and enduring interest in the High North due to Russia's strategic capabilities and activities in the region, and the bilateral relationship between the US and Norway is extremely solid. Some are worried that this might change. President Donald Trump might not only unravel the liberal, rules-based order on which countries like Norway rely; he has also introduced a significant level of animosity and unpredictability between the US and Europe. A deep and irreversible rift would constitute a major challenge to Norwegian security, since only the US has the military muscle to deter Russia in the north. However, it may still be the case that President Trump's agenda is an aberration and not necessarily expressive of a fundamental new reality. The crisis could even be seen as a creative-destructive force that will eventually reinvigorate the transatlantic partnership, notably because Europe will invest more in defence and hence bring about a more equitable burden-sharing.

The turbulent political flows have not been reflected in bilateral military cooperation, which is proceeding on a familiar path and is being expanded in several areas. Cooperation in intelligence and surveillance has grown significantly, and the USAF is improving airbase infrastructure in Norway to sustain its engagement in Northern Europe. Most important, the US Marine Corps is enhancing its engagement in Norway. Under the Marine Corps Prepositioning Program–Norway, vehicles and supplies in mid-Norway have been renewed and tailored to support a Marine Air Ground Task Force (MAGTF) of about 4,500 personnel. If need be, the arrangement could be expanded to facilitate the arrival of an expeditionary brigade of 15,000 to 18,000 troops, which in turn could call for storage of more materiel.

In 2017, the US also deployed a rotational force of approximately 330 marines to the Værnes Air Station in mid-Norway, close to the storage caves. The Marine Corps has signalled from the beginning that it would like to increase its presence in Norway to a battalion-sized force and make it the marines' hub in Europe.[18] While the issue has been politically controversial, the US and Norway agreed in August 2018 to prolong the agreement for another five years, lift the ceiling to 700 marines, and divide their activity between mid-Norway and inner Troms, close to the locations of Norwegian armed forces as well as UK and Dutch marines. The force is a strong security policy signal and underlines the credibility of the guarantee. Critics contend it violates Norway's policy prohibiting the stationing of allied forces, but these are not bases in the traditional sense, nor are they tripwires or reinforcement forces in the manner of an MAGTF. The two locations are hubs used for training and exercises in the harsh northern climate in Norway and in other countries in the region.

The Northern Triangle

While the UK expects to operate in a range of theatres, the 2015 Strategic Defence and Security Review will better prepare it for a role in the North Atlantic and High North. Norway, the US and the UK will operate the same maritime patrol aircraft, the P-8A Poseidon, and they are about to build a trilateral partnership for maritime operations in the North Atlantic. The UK's new *Queen Elizabeth*-class carriers, and the battle groups around them, can significantly contribute to establishing freedom of manoeuvre and supporting force projection in the north, although

---

[18] Tamnes, 'The Significance of the North Atlantic and the Norwegian Contribution', p. 28; Heather A Conley, Jeffrey Rathke and Matthew Melino, *Enhanced Deterrence in the North, A 21st Century European Engagement Strategy* (Washington, DC: CSIS, February 2018).

realistically this would occur only in conjunction with major US deployments. The UK-led Joint Expeditionary Force (JEF), which achieved full operational capability in June 2018, can make a difference in the early stages of a High North contingency. Furthermore, a cluster of amphibious forces is emerging in the north. The UK Royal Marines and the Dutch Korps Mariniers have trained for Arctic warfare in Norway for almost 50 years. From 2018 to 2019, their activity will be concentrated within inner Troms in northern Norway, where they can also train and exercise with the US Marine Corps and the Norwegian armed forces. This will better prepare them for high-intensity operations.[19] Since projecting power from the sea is a demanding task in the highly contested areas in the north, pre-positioned equipment could reduce the force vulnerability, transfer time, and the burden of escorting reinforcement convoys.

The UK and the Netherlands are key states in NATO's maritime strategy, especially on the southernmost point of the Northern Triangle. Although Germany's engagement in the maritime domain is currently mostly confined to the Baltic Sea, it also has the potential to play an important role in the North Sea and the southern Norwegian Sea. Norway's decision in 2017 to acquire German submarines solidifies a strategic partnership which can also strengthen Norwegian defence and foreign policy bonds within Europe. The next logical step should be for the Deutsche Marine to re-engage westwards – similar to how the Bundesmarine did around 1980, when it extended its area of operations beyond the 61st parallel that demarcates the North Sea and the Norwegian Sea. The US Navy normally has a minimal number of capital ships in this region, which leaves European navies, ideally with German participation, with the prime responsibility for confronting Russia in the early phase of a conflict and thereby creating the basis for securing the sea lanes and reinforcing Northern Europe.

Russia's anti-access strategy, and the return of the North Atlantic as a strategic pivot, highlight the significance of Iceland as a point of the Northern Triangle.[20] NATO allies have carried out surveillance and interception flights in Iceland's airspace since 2008. In 2014, the US deployed surveillance and anti-submarine warfare (ASW) aircraft to Iceland in reaction to the crisis with Russia and increased Russian

---

[19] House of Commons, 'Defence Committee, Sunset for the Royal Marines? The Royal Marines and UK Amphibious Capability', Third Report of Session 2017–19, HC 622, 4 February 2018, <https://publications.parliament.uk/pa/cm201719/cmselect/cmdfence/622/622.pdf>, accessed 15 April 2018.

[20] Alyson J K Bailes and Kristmundur Þór Ólafsson, 'Developments in Icelandic Security Policy', *Stjórnmál og stjórnsýsla [Icelandic Review of Politics and Administration]* (Vol. 1, No. 2, 2014), pp 1–16.

submarine activity around the island. Iceland recognises the challenges posed by Russia's activities, but US plans to re-engage also raise Icelandic concerns about entrapment. Iceland has joined in EU and NATO member sanctions against Russia, and although this has proven unpopular because of the heavy cost of Russian counter-sanctions, Iceland has remained firm. Furthermore, in 2016 the Icelandic parliament approved a national security policy – its first ever. It confirms Iceland's participation in NATO and describes the 1951 defence agreement with the US as a pillar of the country's defence. Shortly afterwards, a joint defence agreement with the US reaffirmed both the commitments and obligations of the 1951 agreement and the 2006 'joint understanding' on security cooperation as US forces withdrew from Iceland.[21]

The Iceland Air Defence System, which operates four radar complexes, is being modernised, based on a 2017 NATO decision. NATO and Iceland also have plans for renovating taxiways and aircraft shelters at Keflavik airbase. Iceland is increasing its investments in defence and security to a total of $17.9 million in 2018, but it expects NATO to contribute more to infrastructure in Iceland.

While NATO's contributions demonstrate cohesion and deterrence, US engagement in Iceland makes the difference militarily.[22] The US Navy is using Keflavik more extensively for P-8A surveillance and ASW flights to monitor Russian submarines slipping into the North Atlantic. These are rotational deployments; no serious discussions have addressed a permanent presence that Iceland would find very problematic. The Pentagon budgeted $14.4 million in 2018 to refurbish a hangar and construct a rinse facility at Keflavik. Iceland's bilateral talks with the US have at times been contentious, but cooperation between them is about to become more extensive, including exercises on a regular basis.

The High North and Maritime Strategy

NATO's strategy for the North Atlantic depends on strong naval forces and a command structure matched to its purpose. Some pieces are starting to fall into place; most importantly the approval at the NATO summit in July 2018

---

[21] Government Offices of Iceland, 'Parliament Resolution on a National Security Policy for Iceland', 16 April 2016, <https://www.government.is/media/utanrikisraduneyti-media/media/Varnarmal/National-Security-Policy-ENS.pdf>, accessed 13 July 2018; Government Offices of Iceland, 'Joint Understanding: the Government of the United States of America and the Government of the Republic of Iceland', 29 June 2016, <https://www.government.is/library/01-Ministries/Ministry-for-Foreign-Affairs/Joint_Understanding.pdf>, accessed 13 July 2018.

[22] Gregory Winger and Gustav Petursson, 'Return to Keflavik Station, Iceland's Cold War Legacy Reappraised', *Foreign Affairs*, 24 February 2016.

of a new NATO command structure and maritime posture. However, a number of key pieces are still missing.

An overarching aim of ongoing work is to improve NATO's ability for war-fighting and high-end operations in all of Supreme Allied Commander Europe's (SACEUR) area of responsibility, including the maritime domain. ASW capabilities are crucial to success. Numerically, the Alliance has lost almost half its ASW capability over the last 20 years. One of NATO's key priorities is therefore to regain its advantage in ASW, benefiting from new technologies and non-traditional modes of operation. This would include unmanned autonomous systems, stealth, and endurance, as well as non-acoustic detection and offensive-cyber techniques.[23] NATO's Standing Naval Forces (SNF) are a core maritime capability, but they are small and have declined over recent years. In today's security environment there is a need for larger, high-end maritime groups. Furthermore, carrier-strike power projection is critical, and should be reintroduced in forward areas to demonstrate power and resolve in both peace and war. Twenty-six years have passed since NATO last undertook an exercise in the Norwegian Sea that included a carrier battle group. Deploying carriers has become a more feasible option as US Navy deployments are shifting from predictable, pre-planned routes to shorter, more event-driven deployments. In line with the philosophy of competitive strategy, this will make deployments more unpredictable during peacetime, and readier to surge and deal with high-end warfare. Deterrence should contribute to predictability and stability while also introducing an element of uncertainty in the mind of an opponent.

The US and NATO have come a long way in revamping the command structure for the maritime domain to better prepare for high-end operations. One important step in 2018 has been the reactivation of the US Second Fleet after its disbandment in 2011. Another significant step is the establishment of a NATO Joint Force Command Norfolk for the North Atlantic, while Allied Maritime Command (MARCOM) in Northwood, UK, will be empowered as a maritime-theatre component commander. The new NATO command in Norfolk signifies a promising start to rebuilding the institutional and operational connection between North America and Europe. When activated in a high-end conflict, the command will have specific responsibility for the transatlantic sea lines of communication and the protection of reinforcements to Europe. The next move should be to clarify its responsibility for forward operations. In general, to enhance unity of command, the Alliance needs to more clearly define the roles and

---

[23] Bryan Clark, *The Emerging Era in Undersea Warfare* (Washington, DC: CSBA, January 2015).

responsibilities of the various headquarters, including the extent of engagement in and responsibility for forward operations in the High North.

There is also the potential to further strengthen the regional focus of the joint force command headquarters and also the linkages between NATO's command structure and individual national headquarters with particular regional expertise and situational awareness. For example, the Norwegian national joint headquarters in Bodø in northern Norway has a deeper understanding of the High North and Russian operations than any other command; it is also well adapted to NATO working practices and procedures and has played an important role in NATO exercises based on best practice.

Conclusion

Under Putin's leadership, Russia has reverted to its traditional view of the West characterised by suspicion, ideological distance and strategic conflict of interest. Russia's military build-up in the north and its anti-access strategy accentuate the asymmetric relationship between Norway and Russia, pose a challenge to the transatlantic lifeline, and threaten to undercut North American attempts to reinforce Europe. Containing Russia in the north is therefore of utmost importance, and NATO should view the High North as a strategic flank of both Central Europe and the transatlantic sea lanes.

NATO and some of its key members, notably the US, have returned their attention to the north. They face the difficult task of building credible deterrence and defence. Success will depend on the ability of the Alliance to devise a broad-based response. To compensate for regional asymmetry, NATO should formulate a competitive strategy, capitalising on its own strengths and Russia's weaknesses. In this context, theatre-wide strategies and operations have great potential. First, if NATO clearly perceives the Northern European front line as a whole, from the Baltic to the High North, Russia will have to realise that an isolated assault in the north or in the Baltic will unleash a broad Western response. Second, and equally importantly, NATO must establish a strong bridge between North America and the North European front line. This highlights the significance of bases in the Northern Triangle, and of making NATO's maritime posture and command structure robust enough to deal with high-end conflict. NATO has made remarkable progress in few years, but there is still a long way to go.

II. THE BALTIC REGION

TOMAS JERMALAVIČIUS AND EERIK MARMEI

After the end of the Cold War and the collapse of the Soviet Union, Central and Eastern European states understood that they could only ensure their future security and wellbeing by fully integrating with Western institutions. The Baltic States' accession to NATO and the EU involved a long process that started soon after independence. While their consensus on joining NATO was strong, it was more difficult to secure agreement from existing members. The relatively weak defence capabilities of the Baltic States, Russia's objections to NATO enlargement, and a lack of vision and political will of some Allies were the main obstacles to Baltic membership. For Estonia, Latvia and Lithuania, integration into NATO turned out to be politically a more arduous journey than joining the EU.

Nevertheless, having welcomed Poland, the Czech Republic and Hungary to its ranks at its 1999 Summit in Washington, DC, NATO reaffirmed its commitment to the enlargement process and presented nine aspirant countries – including the three Baltic States – with Membership Action Plans (MAP). In 2002, at its summit in Prague, NATO decided to invite Bulgaria, Estonia, Latvia, Lithuania, Romania, Slovakia and Slovenia to begin accession talks to join the Alliance, which culminated in their membership on 29 March 2004. As a practical manifestation of the benefits of membership and burden-sharing, the Allies immediately launched the Baltic Air Policing (BAP) operation – a peacetime mission to patrol the Baltic States' airspace. Conducted from an airbase in Lithuania, it remained NATO's only form of presence in the Baltics for more than a decade.

Historical experience and concerns about an uncertain future acted as powerful driving forces for the Baltic States to seek stronger protection against threats to their statehood. A common guiding principle of their foreign and security policies since regaining independence has been 'never alone again', which meant that they took a path of full integration into the Western political, economic, security and defence organisations and institutions. The Baltic States have been extraordinarily successful in achieving this goal: as of today, they are members of more Western multinational institutions than most of their Baltic Sea neighbours. However, this was not the 'end of history' in the Baltic quest for security.

This chapter appraises how the Baltic States have responded to Russia's growing geopolitical assertiveness, political warfare and military aggression. It shows how Estonia, Latvia and Lithuania have vigorously pursued the recognition of their security concerns by their allies and partners, as well as sought to leverage their regional cooperation networks as a bulwark against what they perceived as a renewed existential threat posed by the regime in Moscow. It also examines how they have refocused their own defence-development efforts to deal with this threat. Although each Baltic State has its own internal political and societal context, strategic culture and national defence model, this chapter treats them as a cohesive geostrategic region. There are only minor differences in the threat they perceive from Russia and the resulting NATO measures.

The main argument of this chapter is that despite the Baltic States representing a success story of integration with the West, the darkened outlook for regional and transatlantic security places significant new demands on their strategy-making, defence development, and priorities for cooperation. The Baltic States have had to reassess many of their policy assumptions, integration achievements, capability preferences, and cooperative engagements. They will continue to be tested by an overwhelming threat from Russia.

A Changed European Security Landscape

At the same time that the Baltic countries acceded to both NATO and the EU, the first indications emerged that the security situation in Europe was beginning to change. After the 'colour revolutions' in Georgia (2003) and Ukraine (2004), Russia's President Vladimir Putin declared, in 2005, that the collapse of the Soviet Union had been a major geopolitical disaster of the twentieth century. During the Munich Security Conference in 2007, he delivered an infamous speech in which he forcefully criticised the West and blamed the US for undermining global stability.[1] Russia's new strategic planning documents, such as the 2008 Foreign Policy Concept, 2009 National Security Strategy and 2010 Military Doctrine, all

[1] Thom Shanker and Mark Landler, 'Putin Says US is Undermining Global Stability', *New York Times*, 11 February 2007.

demonstrated the return of great-power competition in Russian strategic thinking.[2]

In April 2007, Estonia came under what could be considered the first modern hybrid attack against a state, which combined incitement of street protests by members of a Russophone minority, a massive disinformation campaign, diplomatic and economic coercion, and cyber attacks. Russian military action against Georgia in August 2008 was received with apprehension by the Baltic States, but failed to result in any long-term change in the West's relations with Russia. Following Russia's initial invasion, NATO foreign ministers suspended the NATO-Russia Council (NRC) and halted military-to-military cooperation between NATO and Russia. However, in March 2009, the North Atlantic Council decided to resume NRC meetings, while the US focused on 'resetting' relations with Moscow.[3] The West followed a policy of engagement on issues of perceived shared interest, including challenges such as nuclear disarmament, the war in Afghanistan, and both Iran and North Korea.[4]

In September 2009, during the *Zapad* ['West'] military exercise, Russia purportedly simulated a nuclear strike against and invasion of Poland.[5] This, coupled with the attack on Georgia, spurred a sustained effort by the Baltic States to pressure NATO into developing contingency plans to counter possible Russian aggression. In 2010, after a period of difficult discussions and persistent arguments from the Baltic capitals that they should not be relegated to the status of 'second-class members', NATO adopted formal plans for the defence of the Baltic States and Poland under the name *Eagle Guardian*.[6] Despite this, the US announced the withdrawal of two combat brigades (7,000 troops) from Europe in January 2012.[7] Further evidence of a US drawdown in Europe was demonstrated in the 2013 major NATO exercise *Steadfast Jazz*, when the US contributed with only

---

[2] Riina Kaljurand, 'The Annexation of Crimea and its Implications for the Baltic States' Security', in Andris Kudors (ed.), *Fortress Russia: Political, Economic, and Security Development in Russia Following the Annexation of Crimea and its Consequences for the Baltic States* (Riga: Centre for East European Policy Studies, University of Latvia Press, 2016), p. 171.

[3] Helene Cooper, 'Russia Aims to be High on Obama's Agenda', *New York Times*, 7 November 2008.

[4] Jake Sullivan, 'The Putin Files: The US-Russian Reset', Carnegie Endowment for International Peace, 25 October 2017.

[5] Matthew Day, 'Russia "Simulates" Nuclear Attack on Poland', *The Telegraph*, 1 November 2009.

[6] *The Economist*, 'The Eagle Guardian Has Landed', 7 December 2010.

[7] *BBC News*, 'US to Withdraw Two Europe Combat Brigades', 13 January 2012; Thom Shanker and Steven Erlanger, 'US Faces New Challenge of Fewer Troops in Europe', *New York Times*, 13 January 2012.

160 personnel.[8] The Obama administration's 'pivot to Asia' policy was then in full swing, causing much trepidation in the Baltic capitals.

A fundamental shift in Europe's security and Western policies towards Russia occurred only after the Russian annexation of Crimea and the war launched by Moscow in Eastern Ukraine in spring 2014. The US played a leading role in responding to the Russian actions by bolstering the security of NATO's eastern flank. In June 2014, President Obama introduced the European Reassurance Initiative (ERI) to enhance the US presence in Europe, including a rotational presence of US troops in Poland and the Baltic States.[9] During his visit to Estonia in September 2014, Obama emphasised commitment to NATO's Article 5 and declared that 'the defence of Tallinn and Riga and Vilnius is just as important as the defence of Berlin and Paris and London'.[10]

The Baltic States emerged as prominent voices, calling for stronger collective defence and the adjustment of NATO's posture, particularly by ensuring visible and meaningful presence of Allied forces in the region. The 2014 NATO Summit in Wales produced a plan for a Very High Readiness Joint Task Force (VJTF) and set a goal of at least 2 per cent defence spending for all NATO members by 2024. NATO doubled the size of the BAP, with Ämari airbase in Estonia added to the mission. Building on the Wales Summit promise of military reassurance, the 2016 Warsaw Summit put forward a clear plan for Enhanced Forward Presence (EFP), deploying battalion-size battlegroups – or a tripwire deterrent force – to the Baltic States and Poland. Although this was certainly a welcome development, some cautioned that this 'was not a final destination' and that strengthening of deterrence in the region had to continue.[11]

In addition to conventional military preparedness, NATO sought a joint response with the EU to the various types of hybrid threats. These

---

8 Anna Wieslander, 'NATO, the US and Baltic Sea Security', UIpaper, No. 3, 2016, Swedish Institute of International Affairs, <https://www.ui.se/globalassets/butiken/ui-paper/2016/nato-the-u.s.-and-the-baltic-sea-security—aw.pdf>, accessed 13 July 2018.

9 White House Office of the Press Secretary, 'Remarks by President Obama at 25th Anniversary of Freedom Day', 4 June 2014, <https://obamawhitehouse.archives.gov/the-press-office/2014/06/04/remarks-president-obama-25th-anniversary-freedom-day>, accessed 13 July 2018.

10 White House Archives, 'Remarks by President Obama to the People of Estonia', 3 September 2014, <https://obamawhitehouse.archives.gov/the-press-office/2014/09/03/remarks-president-obama-people-estonia>, accessed 13 July 2018.

11 Wesley Clark et al., *Closing NATO's Baltic Gap* (Tallinn: International Centre for Defence and Security, 2016), <https://www.icds.ee/fileadmin/media/icds.ee/failid/ICDS_Report-Closing_NATO_s_Baltic_Gap.pdf>, accessed 13 July 2018.

are a distinct threat for the Baltic States, and their policies to counter them are regarded as among the most rigorous in the EU.[12] However, the joint Russian–Belarusian Exercise *Zapad* in 2017 once again showed Russian preparedness to challenge NATO militarily.[13] Military power remains the 'hard currency' of security in the region, and the Baltic States are at the forefront of investing in all aspects of military capability.

Baltic Defence Development

In the early years of NATO membership, the defence strategies, force posture and force composition of the Baltic States – especially Latvia and Lithuania – evolved towards deployable light expeditionary capabilities required for NATO and EU operations. In the absence of a perceived military threat to their homeland, and under pressure to increase their contribution to Alliance operations, Latvia and Lithuania moved away from territorial-defence strategies, developed niche specialisations for troop contributions to counterinsurgency and stabilisation operations, and focused on improving their interoperability with NATO systems.[14] In 2006, Latvia suspended military conscription and began relying on an all-volunteer force; Lithuania followed in 2008. Estonia took a distinct path, continuing with military conscription and a mobilisation-based, territorial-defence model.

All three countries eventually became capable of deploying 'company-plus' infantry units on operations, along with some specialised assets including transport aircraft, water purification, de-mining units and special forces. They, of course, heavily depended on Allied or coalition logistical support for sustainment in operations, such as the International

---

12 In the Kremlin Watch's report on the EU-28, the Baltic States, along with Sweden, are classified as 'full-scale defenders' against Russia's hybrid forms of aggression; Finland, Denmark, Germany and Poland are in 'the awakening' group (other groups are 'the mildly concerned', 'the hesitants', 'the ignorants', and the 'Kremlin collaborators'). See European Values, 'Guide to Kremlin's Disinformation and Influence Operations in Europe: Summary of What Every Policy-Maker Should Know', 17 September 2017, <http://www.europeanvalues.net/wp-content/uploads/2017/09/Guide-to-Kremlins-disinformation-influence.pdf>, accessed 13 July 2018.

13 Keir Giles, 'Russia Hit Multiple Targets with Zapad-2017', US-Russia Insight, Carnegie Endowment for International Peace, 25 January 2018, <http://carnegieendowment.org/2018/01/25/russia-hit-multiple-targets-with-zapad-2017-pub-75278>, accessed 13 July 2018.

14 Erik Männik, 'The Evolution of Baltic Security and Defence Strategies', in Tony Lawrence and Tomas Jermalavičius (eds), *Apprenticeship, Partnership, Membership: Twenty Years of Baltic Defence Development* (Tallinn: ICDS, 2013), pp. 13–44.

Security Assistance Force (ISAF) in Afghanistan.[15] Participation in ISAF saw Lithuania take the lead in a Provincial Reconstruction Team and forge very effective special forces, which became a separate service of the Lithuanian Armed Forces in 2008.[16] Estonia continuously contributed an infantry company to one of the most dangerous parts of Afghanistan under UK lead without any national caveats – a rarity among the coalition.[17] In all three countries, such involvement was a major driver of organisational learning and change as well as growing professionalism. However, by and large, the expeditionary era meant the armed forces remained small, light and lacking in a wider range of capabilities.

Russia's aggression against Georgia triggered rethinking of defence strategies in the Baltic capitals. Given the impact of the global financial crisis in 2008, however, the Baltic States were unable to fund any significant investments in defence; indeed, Latvia's and Lithuania's defence budgets slid below 1 per cent of GDP.[18] There was a growing risk that they could, at some point, be seen as under-achievers and free-riders within the Alliance.[19] Estonia was the quickest to rebound to pre-crisis spending levels and achieve the 2 per cent of GDP benchmark on defence spending by 2012. Even then, the available financial resources in absolute terms remained modest and only provided for continuing or initiating few investment projects (for example, short-range air-defence systems and armoured personnel carriers).

Russia's aggression against Ukraine served as a major impetus in reorienting national defence priorities in both Lithuania and Latvia and impelled them to allocate significant resources to defence investment. Since 2014, their defence budgets have been among the fastest growing in the world, doubling in size and being on course to reach (and even exceed) the NATO 2 per cent target by 2018.[20] Collectively, the Baltic

---

[15] Piret Paljak, 'Participation in International Operations', in Lawrence and Jermalavičius (eds), *Apprenticeship, Partnership, Membership*, pp. 202–32.

[16] Lithuanian Armed Forces, 'Special Operations Forces', updated 26 February 2018, <http://kariuomene.kam.lt/en/structure_1469/special_operations_forces.html>, accessed 13 July 2018.

[17] Kadi Salu and Erik Männik, 'Estonia', in Heiko Biehl, Bastian Giegerich and Alexandra Jonas (eds), *Strategic Cultures in Europe: Security and Defence Policies Across the Continent* (Potsdam: Springer VS, 2013), pp. 99–112.

[18] Kristīne Rudzīte-Stejskala, 'Financing Defence', in Lawrence and Jermalavičius (eds), *Apprenticeship, Partnership, Membership*, pp. 189–90.

[19] Kęstutis Paulauskas, 'The Baltic Quest to the West: From Total Defence to "Smart Defence" (and Back?)', in Lawrence and Jermalavičius (eds), *Apprenticeship, Partnership, Membership*, p. 77.

[20] *Baltic Times*, 'Think-Tank: Baltic Defense Budgets are Fastest-Growing Worldwide', 20 October 2016; *Latvian Public Broadcasting,* 'Latvia's Defense Spending will Hit 2% of GDP in 2018', 11 October 2017, <https://eng.lsm.lv/article/

States now spend close to €2 billion on defence annually, with around 20 per cent spent on procurement. This provides for relatively ambitious armament acquisition programmes focused on: armoured manoeuvre and mobility (infantry fighting vehicles); fire support (self-propelled howitzers); anti-armour (anti-tank weapons); short- and medium-range air defence systems; command, control, communications, and information (C3I); intelligence, surveillance and reconnaissance (ISR); logistical support; and other capabilities. Funding growth has also supported the expansion and improvement of infrastructure (including training areas and host-nation support for NATO EFP) and investments in reserve stocks (including ammunition), as well as one of the most intensive training and exercise programmes ever undertaken by the Baltic States.

With a complete reorientation towards homeland defence within the collective defence framework, Lithuania reintroduced conscription in 2015 – the very first NATO member to switch back from an all-volunteer format – and began the process of building up a second brigade.[21] The Latvian and Estonian militaries are undergoing similar expansion, both in personnel numbers and structures. The Estonian Defence Forces, for instance, are also in the process of building up a second brigade and have begun experimenting with cutting-edge concepts and capabilities, reflected in Estonia's ambition to stand up a separate cyber command in 2018.[22] Latvia, however, has retained the all-volunteer format, expecting to recruit and train sufficient numbers of full-time professionals for the Latvian National Armed Forces and territorial-defence volunteers for the Latvian National Guard (Zemessardze).[23]

The sense of an overwhelming and existential military threat from Russia brought the Baltic States to a completely new qualitative and quantitative level of defence development: their armed forces have never been so well resourced, equipped and capable – even bearing in mind that many of their capability investments are yet to fully bear fruit. Despite a shift to homeland defence, they also remain quite actively involved in

---

society/defense/latvias-defense-spending-will-hit-2-of-gdp-in-2018.a253243/>, accessed 8 July 2018; *Baltic Times*, 'Lithuania's 2018 Defense Budget Should be 2.06 pct of GDP', 11 October 2017.

[21] Tomas Jermalavičius, 'Reinstating Conscription in Lithuania: Bringing Society Back into Defence?', in Andris Sprūds and Māris Andžāns (eds), *Security in the Baltic Sea Region: Realities and Prospects* (Riga: Latvian Institute of International Affairs, 2017), pp. 33–53.

[22] International Centre for Defence and Security, 'Estonian National Defence 2022', Seminar at the International Centre for Defence and Security, Tallinn, 22 February 2018.

[23] *Baltic Course,* 'PM Does Not Support Introducing Mandatory Army Conscription in Latvia', 25 February 2015.

international operations to show solidarity with common causes and interests of other NATO allies.[24]

Given Russia's superiority in conventional forces in the region and its anti-access/area denial (A2AD) approach, as well as the unaffordable cost of many high-end defence capabilities (for example, medium- and long-range air defence), the Baltic States will, however, remain highly dependent on NATO, specifically on allies' more substantial rotational presences and reinforcements. Having concentrated on building capabilities in the land domain, the Baltic States have yet to seriously turn their attention to the air or maritime domains. At the same time, this situation should serve as a strong incentive to seek common solutions through various multinational cooperative frameworks to generate, maintain and field a new generation of capabilities across all operational domains.

Multinational Cooperation

Multinational cooperation – regional, European and transatlantic – has been pivotal for the Baltic States. It has been instrumental to their adopting Western leadership and management practices in defence organisations, receiving foreign military assistance, developing their military capabilities, enhancing their interoperability and integrating them with Alliance forces, and gaining practical experience in operations. From the mid-1990s, the Baltic Battalion (BALTBAT), Baltic Naval Squadron (BALTRON), Baltic Air Surveillance Network (BALTNET), and Baltic Defence College (BALTDEFCOL) formed the backbone of trilateral Baltic cooperation and were the main vehicles for engaging NATO and EU partners. Of these, only BALTNET and BALTDEFCOL still exist, while Estonia withdrew from BALTRON and no major initiatives or trilateral programmes have been put in place.[25]

At the same time, the establishment of NATO Centres of Excellence – Cooperative Cyber Defence in Tallinn, Strategic Communication in Riga, and Energy Security in Vilnius – has provided a new framework for multilateral cooperation and the involvement of foreign partners. All three focus on niche competences of growing importance to Alliance security and attract wide participation from as far away as Japan. While not dealing with 'hard' military defence, they are beginning to make an important

---

[24] *Baltic Times*, 'Defmin to Seek Mandate for Estonian Troops' Participation in Africa Mission', 24 January 2018; Fergus Kelly, 'Lithuania to Deploy Special Operations Forces to Afghanistan in NATO Train and Assist Role', *Defense Post*, 22 February 2018.

[25] Uģis Romanovs and Māris Andžāns, 'The Trilateral Military Cooperation of the Baltic States in the "New Normal" Security Landscape', in Sprūds and Andžāns (eds), *Security in the Baltic Sea Region*, pp. 14–22.

contribution to collective NATO capabilities and the national capabilities of participating states.

Within the context of NATO, the Baltic States have also contributed to successive rotations of the NATO Response Force (NRF), briefly using the BALTBAT as a framework to generate their contributions – typically an infantry company, and also assigning some specialised assets such as mine countermeasures (MCM) ships or transport aircraft.[26] Creation of the VJTF has provided another vehicle for supporting NATO's core tasks. However, those remain largely token contributions, given the overwhelming demands placed on the small Baltic forces at home. In this regard, deployment of the EFP battlegroups currently shapes priorities for military cooperation in a very powerful way: each of the Baltic States has developed very strong links with the lead and contributing nations of the EFP battlegroups (UK-led in Estonia, Canada-led in Latvia and Germany-led in Lithuania) deployed on their soil, sometimes to the detriment of their ability to accommodate more diverse military cooperation formats.

While being strong transatlanticists, the Baltic States have nonetheless participated in the EU Common Security and Defence Policy (CSDP) initiatives and contributed to the implementation of the EU Battle Group (EUBG) concept. All three were part of the Nordic Battle Group in 2008 and 2015 (Estonia also in 2011); Lithuania and Latvia, together with Germany and Slovakia, contributed to the Polish-led EUBG in 2010 and, together with Sweden and the Netherlands, participated in the UK-led EUBG in 2013.[27] All three countries signed up to the Permanent Structured Cooperation (PESCO) in 2017 and expressed strong interest in the European Defence Fund. However, although the CSDP provides a format to engage with non-NATO partners and demonstrate appreciation of the need to strengthen European defence capabilities – a goal strongly endorsed at the official level by the Baltic political leadership – it appears to have a lower priority than defence cooperation in the NATO framework or bilateral defence ties with the US.

Cooperation between the Nordic and Baltic states goes back to 1992 when a regional Nordic–Baltic cooperation format was created with the aim of establishing informal high-level political dialogue on regional and international topics. In 2000 this became known as the Nordic–Baltic Eight (NB8). The format, besides hosting foreign- and prime minister-level meetings, has developed several extensions, such as the Enhanced Partnership in Northern Europe (NB8 + US), Nordic Future

---

[26] *Estonian World,* 'Estonia, Latvia, Lithuania to Form Baltic Battalion', 18 November 2013.

[27] Globalsecurity.org, 'EU Battlegroup', <https://www.globalsecurity.org/military/world/europe/eu-battlegroups.htm>, accessed 13 July 2018.

Forum (NB8 + UK), and NB8 + V4 (Visegrad Four: Poland, Czech Republic, Slovakia, Hungary).

At a more practical level, some of the Nordic countries have taken a lead in standing up the Baltic projects (Denmark – BALTBAT, Sweden – BALTDEFCOL and Norway – BALTNET). Their own defence cooperation platform, NORDEFCO, has become open to the participation of the Baltic States – initially through specific areas including veteran affairs, gender issues, and distance learning, but which has broadened across all areas including armament cooperation.[28] However, although NB8 cooperation has greatly enhanced the political dialogue between the participating countries, the fact that Sweden and Finland are not NATO members presents a slight hindrance. The Baltic States seem to be quietly but firmly drawing a 'red line': Sweden and Finland should not be involved in BAP and EFP (in other words, NATO operations).

Still, the Baltic States are very eager to keep both countries as close to NATO as possible, not least because it serves to enhance deterrence in the region and increases the range of options for countering various forms of Russian assertiveness and aggression. The Baltics consider the involvement of Sweden and Finland in Baltic exercises particularly valuable. The air forces of both countries participated in the Baltic Region Training Events (BRTEs) in 2014 and 2015, during which they trained together with the NATO air forces deployed on the BAP. Exercises such as the US-led *Saber Strike* and Estonian *Spring Storm* also started featuring small Swedish and Finnish contingents.[29] Similarly, Sweden hosted troops from the Baltic States in its recent *Aurora* exercise.[30] Such cooperation clearly has both symbolic and practical value, while not diluting NATO's responsibility for collective defence of its members in the region.

In a broader context, the UK-initiated Northern Group (NG) has become one of the vehicles for the Baltic States to informally discuss security and defence issues with like-minded states. At the same time, the notable absence of the US from this forum somewhat diminishes its importance. In November 2017, the NG defence ministers met in Helsinki with US Defense Secretary James Mattis, whose presence showed the

---

28 Pauli Järvenpää, 'NORDEFCO: "Love in a Cold Climate?"', International Centre for Defence and Security, 2017, <https://icds.ee/wp-content/uploads/2017/ICDS_Analysis-NORDEFCO-Pauli_Jarvenpaa-April_2017.pdf>, accessed 13 July 2018.

29 Justyna Gotkowska and Piotr Szymański, *Between Cooperation and Membership: Sweden and Finland's Relations with NATO* (Warsaw: OSW, 2017), pp. 10–11.

30 Mike Winnerstig, 'The Strategic Ramifications of the Aurora 17 Exercise in Sweden', International Centre for Defence and Security Blog, 2 October 2017, <https://icds.ee/the-strategic-ramifications-of-the-aurora-17-exercise-in-sweden/>, accessed 13 July 2018.

potential interest of the US in further developing security cooperation in Northern Europe.[31]

One of the formats where the Baltic States have identified an opportunity to engage more closely with the Nordic countries and some other participants in the NG has been the UK-led Joint Expeditionary Forces (JEF) initiative, which has provided an important vehicle for political-military and military cooperation. Indeed, as some Baltic officials acknowledge, because so many conceptual, policy, legal and military aspects had to be worked out among the participating nations from scratch, JEF has represented a more exciting undertaking than, for instance, the NATO VJTF, which is purely a military project implemented following the Alliance's longstanding force-generation template.[32]

Future Prospects

The Baltic States still have a demanding journey ahead to build their defence capabilities. By 2022–25, many large acquisition programmes launched in recent years will have been completed. This will considerably augment the manoeuvrability, firepower, sustainability and survivability of Baltic forces and their ability to defend their territories in conjunction with the Allies. However, the three states must continue to increase the quantities of armaments coming into service while also remedying remaining capability gaps, or gaps that will appear as existing capabilities reach the end of their life cycle.

It should be perfectly clear to Baltic defence planners that far more trilateral coordination and cooperation in future defence investments is necessary if they are to afford new capabilities. Having missed opportunities for joint procurement of such capabilities as infantry fighting vehicles or self-propelled howitzers – which led to each country simultaneously implementing different solutions – they will have to show much greater willingness and ability to work out common approaches in future programmes. Latvia and Lithuania may be considering joint acquisition of transport/utility helicopters, while all three countries are working together to increase maritime surveillance capabilities. Some officials are beginning to explore the idea of establishing common

---

31 *Politico*, 'Finland Woos US with More Muscular Defense Role', 13 November 2017.

32 Riina Kaljurand et al., *Brexit and Baltic Sea Security* (Tallinn: International Centre for Defence and Security, November 2016), p. 14, <https://icds.ee/wp-content/uploads/2016/ICDS_Report-Brexit_and_Baltic_Sea_Security-November_2016_Final.pdf>, accessed 13 July 2018.

maritime capabilities – even a combined navy – once current platforms are retired.[33]

The US has helped to develop the military capabilities of Estonia, Latvia and Lithuania since independence and NATO membership. Since 2014, the European Reassurance Initiative (ERI) and European Deterrence Initiative (EDI) have provided financial support to the Baltic States and helped to bolster their security, facilitating the US to increase its presence, conduct training and exercises, enhance pre-positioning, improve infrastructure, and build partner capacity. The Baltic States will have to coordinate together and with the US to determine the most important military projects for future EDI funding – around $100 million annually – to address capability, legal and logistics gaps to strengthen their common defence posture.[34]

NATO will play a crucial role in providing more substantial regional capabilities across all domains to deter the threat posed by Russia. Some of those capabilities will continue to be brought in for exercises or during increased regional tensions. Others, however, will have to be stationed more permanently. A multi-layered, integrated air-defence framework will eventually have to be put in place in the region; addressing this issue should involve close cooperation between the Baltic States, Poland and the US. In addition, the Alliance will have to consider transforming the air-policing mission into a more robust air-defence mission.

Given that the bulk of the Alliance's forces will remain concentrated in Western Europe and North America, and behind the so-called Suwalki Gap that runs along the Polish–Lithuanian border between Belarus and Kaliningrad, it will be crucial to remove all obstacles to quick reinforcement of the Baltic States – especially by addressing legal, administrative, diplomatic and infrastructure bottlenecks for cross-border and cross-country movement of military forces. It will also be necessary to enhance early-warning capabilities and the speed of decision-making. NATO, and especially the US, must also consider pre-positioning heavy armament, equipment and supplies in the Baltic States. Finally, the Alliance will have to take a critical look at the remaining gaps in command-and-control (C2) arrangements for the region. Denmark's initiative to establish, together with Latvia and

---

33 International Centre for Defence and Security, 'Estonian National Defence 2022'.

34 Eerik Marmei and Gabriel White, 'European Deterrence Initiative: Bolstering the Defence of the Baltic States', International Centre for Defence and Security, December 2017, <https://icds.ee/wp-content/uploads/2018/05/ICDS_Policy_Paper_European_Deterrence_Initiative_Eerik_Marmei-Gabriel_White_December_2017.pdf>, accessed 13 July 2018.

Estonia as framework states, a multinational division headquarters in Latvia that will be part of NATO's command structure, is an important and welcome step in this direction.[35] However, it will require support and contribution by other nations as well as greater coherence in the Alliance's thinking about C2 arrangements in the region in order to fulfil its potential.

The increased tempo of both national and NATO exercises in the Baltic Sea region gives ample opportunities for maintaining defence linkages with Sweden and Finland. Involving both is important to maintain their familiarity with the Baltic defence and security realities, test interoperability with NATO, develop effective joint crisis-management mechanisms, and prepare both to plug into potential crisis scenarios.

NATO–EU cooperation in a number of areas will be needed to enhance deterrence in the Baltic, from military mobility and infrastructure investment to cyber defence and countering hybrid threats. However, the Baltic States will prefer not to shift the focus of PESCO towards hybrid issues, just as they would not be happy to see PESCO be used to advance defence-industrial protectionism that could undermine transatlantic cooperation. Instead, the Baltic interest in stronger European defence cooperation focuses on cutting-edge solutions to critical military capability shortfalls. Their enthusiasm for deepening defence cooperation within the EU is likely to be determined by the ability of PESCO to finally deliver actual capabilities – particularly those of central importance to regional, European and transatlantic security.[36]

Similar thinking will guide the Baltic approach to greater future involvement in NORDEFCO at the military level: shared strategic understanding, common doctrinal approaches and enhanced capabilities come first. However, there is also a need for greater cooperation on non-military aspects of regional security, including on countering hybrid threats. Situational awareness in various domains, including cyber, and intelligence-sharing and cooperation, must be substantially stepped up across the region. This is where the NB8 and NG – especially if they involve the US and also Canada (given its role on NATO's northern and eastern flanks) – offer important frameworks to develop trust as well as a

---

[35] Danish Ministry of Defence, 'Multinational Division Headquarters in the Baltics', July 2018, <http://www.fmn.dk/temaer/nato/Documents/2018/Multinational-Divisional-Headquarters-in-baltics-NATO-2018.pdf>, accessed 11 July 2018.

[36] Tony Lawrence, Henrik Praks and Pauli Järvenpää, 'Building Capacity for the EU Global Strategy: Companion Report', International Centre for Defence and Security, 2017, <https://icds.ee/wp-content/uploads/2018/ICDS_Policy_Paper_Building_Capacity_for_the_EU_Global_Strategy.pdf>, accessed 13 July 2018.

culture of deeper cooperation. They could and should be extended beyond political and military dimensions to give practical substance to a common understanding of the security challenges already achieved through these and other forums.

III. THE NORDIC REGION

SVEIN EFJESTAD

The Nordic Region is peaceful and prosperous, with few internal or international conflicts. Denmark, Finland, Iceland, Norway and Sweden have many similarities in culture, traditions and social structure. The five countries cooperate extensively in almost all sectors of private and public affairs. The Nordic Council, with its multiple committees and forums at the governmental, ministerial and even parliamentary levels, plays a significant role in promoting cohesion. Although defence is not explicitly a focus of the Nordic Council, the last few years have witnessed increased cooperation in the areas of operations, logistics and information sharing.

The Nordic countries find cooperation valuable as an objective in itself, but especially as a means for strengthening defence within the larger Western security framework. Lately, both Finland and Sweden have deepened their ties with NATO, and the US specifically. Indeed, each of the Nordic countries have strengthened their bilateral relations with each other and other Western states since the Russian annexation of Crimea in 2014.

Prospects for further Nordic cooperation are bright but have limitations in practice as neither Finland nor Sweden is likely to join NATO in the near future. Thus, cooperation will focus on common exercises and training, and on collaboration in international operations and crisis management, while agreements on procurement of military equipment will probably remain relatively rare. This chapter focuses on defence and security cooperation in the Nordic area, providing context, identifying challenges and suggesting possibilities for the way forward.

From Cold War to Cooperation

The five Nordic countries had different security orientations during the Cold War. Negotiations to create a Scandinavian Defence Union in 1948–49 stalled, and Iceland, Denmark and Norway were among the original signatory members of NATO, while Sweden and Finland remained non-aligned and neutral. While the resultant configuration was often called the Nordic Balance, it was by no means a military balance.[1]

During the Cold War, Finland, Sweden, Norway and Denmark maintained large forces based on conscription. Iceland has no military forces of its own; but, in addition to its membership of NATO, it has had a bilateral defence treaty with the US since 1951,[2] under which the US undertakes to defend Iceland. Further, US forces based in Iceland operated from Keflavik airbase during the Cold War. Their main task was surveillance of the North Atlantic, but the base also had an important role as a staging area for reinforcement of continental Europe. In 2006, the permanent stationing of US forces in Iceland ended, but occasional deployments to Keflavik still occurred. Since 2016, military activities in Keflavik have increased again.

Finland signed the Treaty of Friendship, Cooperation and Mutual Assistance with the Soviet Union in 1948.[3] This agreement granted the Soviet Union the right to consult with the Finnish government in certain situations. Western countries, in particular Norway and West Germany, were therefore determined to avoid military moves that could result in Soviet demands for consultations with Finland. As Finland recovered from the Second World War, the situation became more relaxed and Finland gained more freedom to conduct its foreign and security policy without Soviet interference. The treaty was abolished in 1992.

Sweden has a long tradition of neutrality – a policy that has served the country well since the Napoleonic wars. After Sweden and Finland joined the EU in 1994 they moved away from traditional neutrality to non-alignment, but stayed outside military alliances.[4]

Denmark and Norway were solid members of the Western alliance, but did not allow permanent stationing of nuclear warheads or permanent foreign military bases on their territories in peacetime. Greenland was a special case where the US built up an important early warning site at Thule airbase. This installation could again become important as the

---

1 Arne Olav Brundtland, 'Nordisk balanse før og nå' ['The Nordic Balance: Past and Present'], *Internasjonal Politikk* (Vol. 25, No. 5, 1966), pp. 491–541; Johan Jørgen Holst (ed.), *Five Roads to Nordic Security, Norwegian Foreign Policy Studies, 9* (Oslo: Universitetsforlaget, 1973).

2 US Department of State, 'US Relations with Iceland', <https://www.state.gov/r/pa/ei/bgn/3396.htm>, accessed 21 February 2018.

3 Eric Solsten and Sandra W Meditz (eds), *Finland: A Country Study* (Washington, DC: GPO for the Library of Congress, 1988).

4 'Lisbon Treaty', <http://www.lisbon-treaty.org/wcm/the-lisbon-treaty/>, accessed 21 February 2018.

strategic rivalry between Russia and the West grows. Norway also introduced restrictions on allied training, exercises and presence in its most northern county of Finnmark, which has a 196-km border with Russia. These and other restraints were put in place to avoid tension with the Soviet Union and to promote internal consensus, transparency and predictability in security policy. Because these restrictions were self-imposed, the individual governments decided on their interpretation and application. Norway in particular finds it important to cooperate with Russia on fisheries, search and rescue, oil and gas drilling, and general issues in the Arctic. Norway has had '1,000 years of peace' with Russia and the people-to-people relations remain strong in the border region.

The Nordic region represented a strategically important area during the Cold War. Free passage through the Danish straits was crucial for all states with a Baltic coastline. The military importance was obvious: at the time NATO focused on the defence of West Germany and Denmark, and the Baltic Sea constituted the northwestern flank in this regard. Control of Norwegian and Icelandic territory was necessary to maintain control of the North Atlantic and keep the sea lanes of communication open. From the 1960s on, the Kola Peninsula became the base for the Soviet Union's biggest second-strike capability, an essential element in the strategic balance.

In the first two decades after the Cold War, the Nordic countries changed their focus from territorial defence to participation in crisis-management operations. Finland was the only Nordic state that maintained a large mobilisation force based on universal conscription. Denmark, Norway and Sweden maintained much smaller forces, primarily tailored for participation in operations far from home.

During this period, bilateral relationships between the individual Nordic countries and Russia grew closer in defence as well as in other areas. Bilateral contact included high-level visits, exchange of information and participation in training and small exercises. The bilateral defence ties between the Nordic countries and the leading Western powers consisted largely of activities related to materiel acquisition and participation in international operations. Even most multilateral military exercises in the Nordic region concentrated on international crisis-management scenarios.

Defence and Security Cooperation Within the Nordic Area

In 2009, Nordic defence ministers decided to unite different aspects of defence cooperation under one organisational framework: Nordic Defence Cooperation (NORDEFCO). Each of the four lead countries chairs NORDEFCO on a rotational basis. The permanent areas of interest are policy and operations, armament cooperation and capability. Each area has a representative from each state. The Political Steering Committee (PSC) meets twice a year in joint sessions and in separate sessions for each subject area. NORDEFCO also has a military committee that oversees military projects and has organised working groups for training and exercises, capabilities, operations, and other areas. While NORDEFCO serves as a broad framework for Nordic defence cooperation, Nordic countries have no plans to make it a permanent organisation with headquarters and staff.

NORDEFCO has established an effective classified communications network that links all Nordic countries and facilitates rapid communication in times of crisis. Because all five Nordic states are relatively small and vulnerable to changes in the international system, they gain particular value from discussing how small countries could act to achieve their security goals collectively, at home and abroad.

At least seven elements of NORDEFCO merit careful attention.[5] First, the *policy* discussions within NORDEFCO are of great political importance and contribute to significant commonality in the formulation of threat perceptions and challenges. In 2015, the five Nordic states announced their intention to extend their military cooperation in a joint article in the Norwegian newspaper *Aftenposten*.[6] The agreement and the declaration were a direct answer to assertive Russian conduct in the Nordic region.

Second, NORDEFCO members *exchange information* and assessments at all levels. Analysis of changes in the international security environment forms the basis of long-term defence planning, bilateral interactions, participation in international organisations, and formulation of national security policy. Over time, close interaction and consultation among the Nordic countries have resulted in a large degree of commonality in the assessment of international security, including of the UN, NATO, the EU, and other international organisations. Such dialogue promotes common perceptions of long-term developments and new and emerging security issues. The European Centre of Excellence for Countering Hybrid Threats in Helsinki allows Nordic countries to cooperate and prepare to protect against these innovative methods.[7] The NATO Cooperative Cyber Defence Centre of Excellence in Tallinn has

---

5 NORDEFCO, 'NORDEFCO Annual Report 2016', <http://www.nordefco.org/files/NORDEFCO-annual-report-2016.pdf>, accessed 13 July 2018.

6 *Aftenposten*, 'Fem nordiske ministre i felles kronikk: Russisk propaganda bidrar til å så splid' ['Five Nordic Ministers in a Joint Article: Russian Propaganda Contributes to Divisions'], 9 April 2015.

7 Finnish Ministry of the Interior, 'European Centre of Excellence for Countering Hybrid Threats Starts Operating in Helsinki', 1 September 2017, <http://intermin.fi/en/article/-/asset_publisher/eurooppalaisen-hybridiosaamiskeskuksen-toiminta-kaynnistyy-helsingissa>, accessed 21 February 2018.

representatives from all Nordic countries. The Nordic countries have also conducted table-top war-gaming exercises.[8] NORDEFCO also has a military coordination and cooperation group, with each nation represented at the two-star level. This group oversees military working groups in five areas: armaments, capabilities, human resources and education, operations and training, and exercises. These groups organise and arrange many of the more concrete activities in NORDEFCO.

Third, cooperation has promoted *technological interoperability*. Sweden and Finland have gradually improved their interoperability through participation in international peace operations. They have in essence adopted NATO procedures and standards, and today their systems meet NATO interoperability standards better than the systems of some NATO members. Training, exercises and cooperation within the Nordic arena have facilitated and reinforced this development.

Fourth, *cross-border training* for air forces in the north has proven the most successful activity of military cooperation in the NORDEFCO framework. This bottom-up initiative by the air forces of Norway, Sweden and Finland provides an effective training environment for air forces with different equipment and experience. Crews of Swedish Gripens, Finnish F/A-18s and Norwegian F-16s train together weekly, without bureaucratic or political interference, and all gain proficiency by flying against different types of aircraft. This also produces a high degree of interoperability. The biannual *Arctic Challenge* air exercise is an offshoot of this activity and now represents one of the biggest and most complex air exercises in Western Europe,[9] in which close partners such as the US, France and the UK have participated. The Nordic ministers of defence have agreed to develop *Arctic Challenge* further into a flag exercise, which in time might become even more complex and demanding.[10]

Fifth, as Western countries have again shifted their attention to territorial defence, they have discovered the difficulties involved in transporting military forces to and across borders in Europe and have begun new initiatives to reduce bureaucratic restrictions within and

[8] Michael Jari, 'Decision Taken to Create Common Nordic Exercise Plan', Swedish Armed Forces, 17 October 2011 (updated 8 July 2013), <https://www.forsvarsmakten.se/en/news/2011/10/decision-taken-to-create-common-nordic-exercise-plan/>, accessed 21 February 2018.

[9] Norwegian Armed Forces, 'The Third Biennial Arctic Challenge Exercise', <https://forsvaret.no/en/press/the-third-biennial-arctic-challenge-exercise>, accessed 21 February 2018.

[10] *Ibid*.

between countries. Under NORDEFCO's Easy Access initiative,[11] defence ministers have agreed to put in place new procedures that make it possible to transport military forces across borders at short notice. This project will improve the ability of the Nordic countries to cooperate in a flexible and effective way – a key element of both Norwegian and Swedish concepts of 'total defence', which include civil-military cooperation and supply from commercial to defence sectors. Another new project, Nordic Enhanced Cooperation on Air Surveillance (NORECAS), focuses on cooperation in air surveillance in peacetime and contributes to improving interoperability and situational awareness.[12] Once NORECAS is implemented, the Nordic states will be able to exchange air-surveillance data and expand their oversight over their airspace.

Sixth, as previously noted, the Nordic countries have long cooperated in the framework of *international peace operations* and have a standard procedure for ensuring that consultation and coordination take place prior to sending forces to an international operation. Cooperation could involve common transport and support, building of common infrastructure, rotational arrangements to establish enduring force contributions, common training and preparations, and integrated military units.

Finally, cooperation under NORDEFCO extends to *military equipment*, although this presents challenges. The operational environment on the North Atlantic coast is very different from the situation in the Baltic. Denmark and Norway, for example, must take into consideration the close partnership with NATO. Industrial and economic interests play a prominent role, and timing is important. Larger capability-development or investment projects normally have a basis in a white paper agreed on by governments, but so far attempts to coordinate these long-term planning documents have failed. Working together on long-term defence plans could facilitate the development of joint acquisition or joint development of new materiel.

The Nordic nations also increasingly engage in bilateral and trilateral cooperation – some, but not all, under NORDEFCO. Most prominent is cooperation between Sweden and Finland, which has led Stockholm and Helsinki to launch similar initiatives. Both states are 'Enhanced Opportunity' partners of NATO; they have entered into Host Nation Support agreements with NATO, are associated with NATO Readiness

---

[11] NORDEFCO, 'Memorandum of Understanding on Easy Access Signed by Nordic Defence Ministers', <http://www.nordefco.org/Memorandum-of-Understanding-on-Easy-Access-signed-by-Nordic-Defence-Ministers>, accessed 21 February 2018.

[12] NORDEFCO, 'NORDEFCO Annual Report 2016', <http://www.nordefco.org/files/NORDEFCO-annual-report-2016.pdf >, accessed 21 February 2018.

Forces, and participate in the German-led Framework Nation Concept and the UK-led Joint Expeditionary Force. They have entered into similar bilateral agreements with larger Western countries and are adjusting their legislation so they can provide military assistance to other countries and receive military assistance if needed. Swedish–Finnish cooperation also includes contingency planning and mutual exercises.

The Nordic states do not see NORDEFCO as an alternative to NATO or the EU. Intra-Nordic efforts will therefore always be additions and complements to the larger institutional framework for security cooperation.

Nordic Defence Cooperation in the Broader International Context

The Nordic states have traditionally placed strong emphasis on participation in UN peacekeeping. Practical cooperation in support of such missions did not in any way challenge the individual security orientation of each state. UN and Nordic cooperation were always a popular element in the defence policy of all Nordic countries.

With the end of the Cold War, the Nordic states proved willing to allocate forces to UN-authorised NATO operations. This re-energised Nordic military cooperation in order to facilitate joint contributions to peace operations, and included planning, training and intelligence, as well as operations. Focus shifted to the Nordic Coordinated Arrangement for Military Peace Support (NORDCAPS).[13] The Nordic–Polish Brigade in Bosnia and Herzegovina was a noteworthy and visible expression of the increased level of Nordic cooperation.[14] The *Nordic Peace* series of exercises represented an attempt to prepare troops for this task, but proved ineffective and unnecessary. The Nordic ministers of defence then agreed to expand Nordic military cooperation primarily through participation in larger multinational exercises such as *Cold Response*, *BALTOPS* and NATO exercises.

Later, the formation of a Nordic Battle Group as part of EU readiness to engage in peace operations was an expression of increased ambitions and commitment to cooperation.[15] The Nordic Battle Group is considered a Nordic project even though Denmark does not participate because of its reservations regarding defence cooperation within the EU, and some countries outside the Nordic area also contribute forces. The

---

[13] Bengt Holmen and Ståle Ulriksen, 'Norden i felt: På oppdrag for FN og NATO' ['The Nordic Region: On Behalf of the UN and NATO'], Norwegian Institute of International Relations (NUPI), November 2000.

[14] Henning A Frantzen, *NATO and Peace Support Operations 1991-1999: Policies and Doctrines*, Cass Series on Peacekeeping (Abingdon: Taylor and Francis, 2004).

[15] Janne Haaland Matlary and Øyvind Østerund (eds), *Denationalisation of Defence: Convergence and Diversity* (London: Routledge, 2007).

Norwegian and Swedish chiefs of defence proposed a series of initiatives to strengthen bilateral relations in 2007 and 2008, but few if any were implemented.[16]

In the same timeframe, Nordic foreign ministers asked former Norwegian minister Thorvald Stoltenberg to study the possibilities for enhanced cooperation in foreign affairs and security policy. His 2009 report stimulated debate and drew strong political support, although the thirteen concrete proposals in the report had little practical impact.[17] However, today there is considerable Nordic cooperation on participation in international peace operations, training and exercises, capability development, veterans' affairs, and common materiel acquisition. There are also ongoing attempts to coordinate supplies procurement and other aspects of 'total defence' planning. Finland, Sweden and the US signed a new trilateral agreement in May 2018 to improve practical defence cooperation on exercises, situational awareness and interoperability, demonstrating Finnish and Swedish defence coordination with third parties.

Traditionally, Denmark has been less engaged in Nordic defence cooperation and more inclined to engage directly with Western powers. It has committed substantial forces to international operations together with the US and the UK. Denmark did, however, engage strongly in the Nordic–Polish Brigade in Bosnia and Herzegovina. This underlines the Danish priority given to international operations regardless of the framework of force contribution. However, the current defence agreement between Danish political parties, covering the period from 2018–23, is more about the requirements of regional security and collective defence. Support to the Baltic States is high on the Danish defence agenda. Hence, Denmark is now also more engaged in Nordic cooperation.

Most defence cooperation in the Nordic region takes the form of bilateral arrangements or arrangements made outside the Nordic framework. Extensive programmes of cooperation between Finland and Sweden cover contingency planning, training and exercises, and other relevant issues to bolster each nation's defences. The same applies to some extent to other Nordic joint activity. Individual nations arrange exercises and invite Nordic and other Western countries to participate, as in the *Cold Response* exercises (Norway) and the *Aurora* exercise

[16] Håkon Lunde Saxi, 'Nordic Defence Cooperation after the Cold War', Oslo Files 1/2011, March 2011.

[17] Thorvald Stoltenberg, 'Nordic Cooperation on Foreign and Security Policy', 9 February 2009, <https://www.regjeringen.no/globalassets/upload/UD/Vedlegg/nordicreport.pdf>, accessed 21 February 2018.

(Sweden).[18] The US-led *BALTOPS* exercise and the German-led *Northern Coast* exercise also provide opportunities for countries in the Northern Region to improve interoperability and common approaches to operations. The Nordic countries contribute substantial forces to these exercises and these joint and combined military activities reinforce the overall perception and purpose of Nordic cooperation.

Together, the Nordic countries have substantial forces and substantial defence establishments, and therefore the leading Western powers have shown an interest in developing contacts and cooperation with them. The five Nordic countries also represent a political grouping with high standing and influence, and therefore a desirable international partner in general. Through training, exercises and other interactions, Finland and Sweden have achieved a very high degree of interoperability with NATO. This is useful not only in current peace operations, but also if a military crisis should develop in Northern Europe.

The Nordic countries have a close connection with the three Baltic States and hold a joint Nordic–Baltic Ministerial Session once a year, as well as a yearly meeting between the eight nations at the PSC level. The Nordic–Baltic agenda covers a range of different issues, from political consultation to the Nordic–Baltic Assistance Programme.[19] In 2011, the UK initiated the formation of the Northern Group, which also includes Germany, Poland and the Netherlands. The Northern Group meets back-to-back with the ministerial-level NORDEFCO meeting once a year and once a year in connection with other international meetings.[20] The US secretary of defense, NATO secretary general, and other prominent representatives of the international security community attend these meetings. Russian defense ministers have attended past Nordic ministerial meetings. NORDEFCO has thus provided a venue for broader North European security discussions and coordination.

Strategic Considerations

Today, when relations between the West and Russia are more strained than at any time since the end of the Cold War, access to and potential use of the territories of the Nordic countries are again of great strategic importance to both NATO and Russia. This has implications for wartime planning,

---

[18] Heather A Conley (ed.), *Enhanced Deterrence in the North* (Washington, DC: Center for Strategic and International Studies, 2018).

[19] NORDEFCO, 'NORDEFCO Annual Report 2016'.

[20] Swedish Government, 'The Nordic Countries Agree on Deepened Military Cooperation', <http://www.government.se/articles/2016/11/nordefco/>, accessed 21 February 2018.

investments and daily military activities in and around the Nordic area. Russia's more aggressive foreign and security policy is a concern in all Nordic capitals, and the Russian military build-up has political and military implications for the Nordic states, both individually and collectively. As a result, the Nordic countries have individually changed their strategic calculations and assessments. The Nordic governments do not see Russia as a threat, but realise that their national defences and readiness posture must improve, and that their defence and deterrence posture must be adequate to cope with new security challenges in areas surrounding the Nordic countries.

The shortest distance between central Russia and the US lies across Scandinavia and the Arctic. This is significant in relation to perceptions of threat and planning for territorial defence, particularly in the context of strategic nuclear planning and early warning. Russia has heavily concentrated its defences in the north to secure its strategic submarine forces based on the Kola Peninsula. This 'bastion defence' concept would challenge Norwegian territorial sovereignty and access to north Norway in a crisis or war. The nuclear strategic forces, early warning and air defences stationed on the Kola Peninsula clearly demonstrate the emphasis that Russia gives to this area in its defence plans. Conversely, the Russian perception of vulnerability in this region could trigger offensive actions at the expense of the Nordic countries, particularly Norway, in situations of international tension. This region is also relevant in considerations of conventional military operational options. Russia views the Baltic region as crucially important to the defence of Russia and the protection of Russian interests. The Kaliningrad exclave and the coastline around St Petersburg serve as Russia's gateway to Western Europe, especially since the collapse of the Soviet Union. Russia has considerable historical experience of war and invasion from the West, and this history profoundly influences the mindset of Russian authorities; threat perceptions still seem to focus on a scenario in which the West could launch cruise missiles against Russia from the north or northwest. This has shaped Russian military investments and activities around the Nordic region. Russia's leaders are also very sensitive to any missile-defence activity in the northern region because they believe such defences could threaten their country's strategic-strike capabilities. For example, during the Moscow Security Conference in 2011, the Russian chief of the general staff, Yuri Baluyevsky, presented a video of a strategic Russian missile being shot down from a position in the Norwegian Sea. Russian representatives continue to voice concern about NATO's missile defence plans, despite NATO reassurances that its missile defence capabilities will not be directed against Russia.

For NATO and the West, it is imperative to be able to assure sea control in the North Atlantic, which constitutes the transport link for supplies and reinforcement between North America and Europe. Russia could choose to cut or disturb the sea lanes of communication to a degree where North American reinforcement to Europe would be impossible or would arrive too late to be relevant in a conflict.

NATO is also responsible for effective collective defence of Poland, Estonia, Latvia and Lithuania. Effective deterrence and defence in the Baltic region are essential to NATO's overall credibility and to the credibility of the US guarantee to NATO's European members. The overwhelming majority of the economic activity and populations of Sweden, Finland and Denmark are concentrated in the Baltic region or the Baltic approaches. The close partnership that Sweden and Finland have developed with the major Western powers and NATO are important elements in a policy to boost deterrence and defence of their own territory.[21] The Enhanced Opportunity partnership has also led to host-nation support agreements that will facilitate rapid military cooperation when political authorities decide it is necessary.

The Future of Nordic Defence and Security Cooperation

The Nordic states are heavily interlinked across the public and private spheres. This mutual dependence raises wider questions relating to security cooperation. Modern societies are vulnerable to hybrid warfare and to cyber attacks, and Nordic societies rely heavily on imports. It would therefore seem logical to extend existing cooperation to include a 'total defence' concept; in fact, it is difficult to envisage such cooperation without military implications. The new focus on contingency planning demands a comprehensive approach. Protection and supply of civilian societies must be an integral part of the national defence concept, and this requires Nordic cooperation.

As described above, the Nordic countries exhibit a strong sense of solidarity, as well as readiness to exploit opportunities for even closer partnership in the future. They have shown a will to strengthen participation in international operations and to make more common force contributions. Standardisation, training and interoperability will remain important, and issues relevant to modern capabilities, including unmanned and autonomous systems and use of space, are already on the

21 NATO, 'Relations with Sweden', <https://www.nato.int/cps/ic/natohq/topics_52535.htm>, accessed 21 February 2018; NATO, 'Relations with Finland', <https://www.nato.int/cps/ic/natohq/topics_49594.htm>, accessed 21 February 2018.

agenda. Nordic cooperation may also gradually come to include research and development.

In the future, the defence and security policies of the five Nordic countries will likely exhibit many commonalities. In the near term, Nordic cooperation will likely develop within the framework of larger international organisations, primarily NATO, the EU and the UN. Sweden and Finland will likely maintain their active enhanced opportunity partnership with NATO, with a focus on attracting Allied military capability to the Baltic region and thereby improving defence and deterrence in the region and in Northern Europe more generally. However, integration at the policy level will remain limited as long as Finland and Sweden are not members of NATO.

Conclusion

The Nordic members of NATO will continue to have the same general policy objectives, although Norway and Iceland devote special attention to the North Atlantic. Norway, Denmark and Iceland will continue to facilitate Swedish and Finnish cooperation and partnership with NATO, and support their participation in training, exercises and political consultation. Close interaction with NATO will make it possible for all Nordic states to operate alongside forces from NATO member countries at short notice, as decided by the political authorities responsible.

In peacetime, Nordic cooperation will focus on continuing efforts to improve defence capabilities and deterrence and ensure stability and predictability in the region. Should a crisis occur in Northern Europe, there is every reason to believe that the Nordic countries will engage in close consultation and cooperation to shape their response. Acting as a cohesive group will extend the influence and impact of their individual capabilities in contributing to a resolution.

IV. THE UK AND THE NORTHERN GROUP: A NECESSARY PARTNERSHIP

PETER ROBERTS

Between late 2017 and early 2018, the UK prime minister, the secretary of state for defence, chief of the Defence Staff and chief of the General Staff all stated that Russia constitutes the primary security threat facing the UK. This signals a deliberate shift from the preoccupation with violent extremism and terrorism that has dominated UK views on defence for more than two decades.[1]

The UK's armed forces have been increasingly engaged in actions designed to counter Russian aggression in continental Europe, the High North and the Atlantic Ocean. The participation of the RAF as part of the Baltic Air Policing mission on an annual rotation, the deployment of significant elements of the Royal Navy to the Baltic Sea, the redeployment of forces to Norway as part of NATO exercises, and the presence of British Army soldiers and weapons in Estonia as part of the NATO Enhanced Forward Presence mission are all clear indicators of the emphasis being placed on a military counter to Russian actions and growing influence. The armed forces have formed new military groupings, such as 77 Brigade, specifically to counter Russian activities. At the political level, since 2016 both formal reports by parliamentary bodies and more generic inquiries about threats facing the UK have highlighted Russian activities in the North Atlantic and

---

1 *RT*, 'UK PM May Calls Russia "Chief Threat" amid Abysmal Domestic Ratings', 14 November 2017; *Sky News*, 'UK's Undersea Cables at Risk of "Potentially Catastrophic" Attack by Russians', 15 December 2017; Andrew MacAskill, 'UK Sees Growing Threat from Russia Propaganda, Cyber-Attacks', *Reuters*, 18 December 2017; Ewen MacAskill, 'Russia is Biggest Threat to UK Since Cold War, Says Head of British Army', *The Guardian*, 22 January 2018.

the Arctic.[2] The UK has led in imposing economic and political sanctions against Russia since 2014.[3] UK diplomatic relations with Moscow have deteriorated steadily since 2008: the first visit of a UK foreign secretary to Russia in five years (December 2017) has not changed the formal position of either party.[4] Thus, to describe the contemporary attitude of the UK towards Russia as 'cool' would be typical British understatement.

The UN and the EU may have acted as umbrellas for some of these British actions, but NATO has once more dominated as the organisational lynchpin for British responses. Interestingly, however, the UK has also placed increasing emphasis on the relatively new Northern Group as a second structure in which it is aiming to deliver security in a focused area of Europe separate to NATO's geographic span.

Understanding why the UK has chosen to broaden its security linkages beyond the large, established alliances, and develop and integrate its military capability with a group of states that have a range of affiliations with established alliances is important. A Center for Strategic and International Studies paper suggests that this new structure is part of a pattern that constantly reconstructs complex relationships within NATO and that it underscores the inadequacy of and lack of confidence in existing structures (and Article 5 of the Washington Treaty).[5] Such an argument resonates with some commentators in London, and the success of the Joint Expeditionary Force (JEF) – the military alliance that places the majority of the members of the Northern Group as its core contributors of military power – highlights the contrasting commitment of its member states. While the UK continues to make clear public statements about the enduring nature of its relationship with NATO, the relatively rapid pace and tempo of planning, activity and exercises within the JEF is in marked contrast to wider NATO procedures, such as the Alliance's Operational Planning Process. Some might hope that the JEF

---

[2] House of Commons Defence Committee, 'Russia: Implications for UK Defence and Security', HC 107, June 2016, <https://publications.parliament.uk/pa/cm201617/cmselect/cmdfence/107/107.pdf>, accessed 13 July 2018; House of Commons Foreign Affairs Committee, 'The United Kingdom's Relationship with Russia', HC 120, February 2017, <https://publications.parliament.uk/pa/cm201617/cmselect/cmfaff/120/120.pdf>, accessed 13 July 2018.

[3] HM Government, 'Doing Business in Russia and Ukraine: Sanctions Latest', 16 September 2014, <https://www.gov.uk/government/news/doing-business-in-russia-and-ukraine-sanctions-latest>, accessed 13 July 2018.

[4] David Cameron and Barack Obama, 'We Will Not be Cowed by Barbaric Killers', *The Times*, 4 September 2014.

[5] Heather Conley, Jeff Rathke and Mathew Melino, *Enhanced Deterrence in the North: A 21st Century European Engagement Strategy* (Washington, DC and Lanham, MD: CSIS and Rowman & Littlefield, 2018).

and the Northern Group may actually represent a trend for NATO as a whole: a group of states with well-trained, high-readiness forces, able to deploy and make decisions and 'deliver performance at the speed of relevance', built around a framework country and able to include non-NATO members.[6]

This chapter analyses the British perspective on security in Northern Europe by examining events, policies and attitudes that culminated in the decisions to formally advance the Northern Group within NATO and to create the JEF, alongside air- and land-force deployments in the Baltic States and Eastern Europe. It briefly examines institutions alongside NATO as security and defence policy drivers for the UK today, before drawing conclusions about the decisions that future UK governments might take to maintain security in Northern Europe.

A History of the UK and Continental Defence

Many Britons may not actually regard themselves as Europeans. Indeed, the popular media often reflects a strained relationship between the British and their European neighbours. The relationship between the UK and continental Europe reflects a complex dynamic that few acknowledge or understand, but might be described as one in which the UK considers itself the strategic balancer that maintains the status quo on the continent. The English Channel has provided a natural physical barrier to the security concerns of the continent, and there is broad acknowledgement within the UK of the importance of the US and other Anglophone countries; the British public shows less interest in continental European political affairs than in US politics. Although connectivity – both physical through the Channel Tunnel, and economic through continental trade – has improved, this has not overcome the distinct feeling of cognitive dissonance with European thinking and activities. Yet the UK has always played a role in European affairs, whether specifically related to defence and security or at the higher level of great-power politics. The Brexit negotiations between the UK and the EU Commission so far indicate this will continue. To understand this decidedly peculiar relationship, and thus why the UK has decided to invest in an alternative structure, it is vital to reflect on the history of the UK–Europe conundrum.

According to David Stevenson, in many ways the UK did not consider itself part of Europe before 1914: it was an empire in its own right and not simply subject to the laws and behaviours of Europeans, as evidenced, for example, by English actions in the contexts of the Reformation and the

[6] Kori Schake, 'Mattis's Defense Strategy is Bold', *Foreign Policy*, 22 January 2018.

law of the sea.[7] The UK has always held distinctive views on European affairs, and an interest in stability – but strategic stability in the neighbourhood was the priority, rather than dealing with minor border disputes. To the British, the physical barrier of the English Channel between England and France constituted a geographic but also a psychological barrier that led them to see the European continent and its people as foreign and distant.[8] The sea-going English created a navy and prospered, building an empire for trade, becoming rich and thus a target for European states seeking to increase their own wealth. Reliant on trade, raw materials and industry abroad, the UK could not simply ignore Europe: the states on the continent were potentially militarily threatening as well as economic competitors, and they were close enough to be able to invade should the will arise.

As a result, the UK engaged in Europe as the 'strategic balancer', ensuring that no one power became too powerful by arranging pacts and treaties and financing other countries in their inter-state wars.[9] When the UK did engage, it tended to be on a small scale, providing what it considered worthwhile (but expendable) forces in support of one party or another.

The world wars, largely but not exclusively waged in Europe, changed that dynamic. The need for standing armies, as well as continued naval pre-eminence, forced the British public to become deeply embroiled in European events, with many UK citizens travelling to the continent for the first time and expanding their knowledge and understanding of their neighbours. Yet during both wars, the British population relied heavily on non-European goods. American supplies augmented those from the Empire, resulting in a population more familiar with Indian and American products than those from Europe.[10] If anything, Europe seemed less familiar to Britons than countries much more distant.

---

[7] Professor David Stevenson holds the Stevenson Chair in International History at the London School of Economics and Political Science. His publications include: *Armaments and the Coming of War: Europe, 1904–1914* (Oxford: Oxford University Press, 1996); *1914–1918: The History of the First World War* (London: Allen Lane, 2004); *With Our Backs to the Wall: Victory and Defeat in 1918* (London: Allen Lane, 2011); see also Jonathan Ziskind, 'International Law and Ancient Sources: Grotius and Selden', *Review of Politics* (Vol. 35, No. 4, 2015), pp. 537–59.

[8] See Eve Darian-Smith, *Bridging Divides: The Channel Tunnel and English Legal Identity in the New Europe* (Berkeley, CA: University of California Press, 1999); Bojana Perisic, 'Britain and Europe: A History of Difficult Relations', Institute for Cultural Diplomacy, March 2010, <http://www.culturaldiplomacy.org/pdf/case-studies/cs-bojana-perisic>, accessed 13 July 2018.

[9] Ernest Petric, *Foreign Policy: From Conception to Diplomatic Practice* (Leiden: Koninklijke Brill NV, 2013).

[10] Derek Howard Aldcroft, *The European Economy, 1750–1914: A Thematic Approach* (Manchester: Manchester University Press, 1994).

In policy terms, a peaceful continent remained a critical requirement for a peaceful and prosperous UK after each war. Yet the costs of those wars also led to the country's economic downfall. With poorly spent Marshall Plan funding for the UK after 1945, and an empire that began to break apart, recovery was slower than on the continent and the UK continued to incur high costs in terms of maintaining a force in Germany and repaying war debt to the US. British industry continued to rely on Victorian-era infrastructure while the continent flourished under determined leadership.[11] Travel to the continent once more became too expensive for the vast majority of Britons not on military duty.

Closer ties to the US, perhaps united more by a common language and certain personalities rather than shared values, were found on military ties and intelligence sharing, mutual trust and an alignment of interests. The US–UK special relationship, and their reliability as steadfast partners in security matters, did much to underpin the UK's continued presence at the top table.

The Soviet threat and the Warsaw Pact in the 1940s and 1950s focused on British defence thinking and policy. Despite the emergence of the US as the guarantor of security in Europe, the UK continued to regard itself as *primus inter pares* of European powers and was a founding member of NATO. Over the 1960s and 1970s, British defence doctrine gradually reduced the emphasis on overseas commitments and deployments outside Europe, focusing defence spending on an army and air force capable of deterring the Soviet Union and keeping the peace. Naval forces became increasingly concerned with delivering and protecting the sea-based nuclear deterrent submarines, containing the Soviet submarine threat, ensuring the sea lanes of communication with the US remained open and being ready to reinforce Norway against a potential invasion from the forces of the USSR.

At the same time, the establishment of a professional and well-equipped British Army on the Rhine, with supporting RAF cover, increasingly drew on Treasury resources. Over time, the UK abandoned its large carrier force; expertise in anti-submarine warfare with ships, submarines and specialist aircraft became the Royal Navy's key role. The European threat dictated British defence spending, policy and missions: NATO membership was the core of UK defence policy and public discussion, focused on the first line of defence ashore and at sea.[12]

---

[11] Michael Holm, *The Marshall Plan: A New Deal for Europe* (London: Taylor and Francis, 2016).

[12] Robert Self, *British Foreign and Defence Policy Since 1945: Challenges and Dilemmas in a Changing World* (London: Macmillan, 2010).

In 1982, the UK responded to the Argentine invasion of the Falkland Islands by deploying a self-sustaining force of land, sea and air forces to the islands, around 8,000 miles from the British Isles. The failure of key allies to render support shocked the British establishment and the military: France's sale of Exocet missiles to Argentina, and the absence of US political or military support ran counter to all British presumptions of strong relationships and alliances.[13]

Also in 1982, but in Germany rather than the South Atlantic, the British Army started to embrace new military doctrine alongside new capabilities: the arrival of precision-guided munitions heralded the arrival of new technology on a battlefield that had previously been highly reliant on mass of arms and fighting spirit. The British quickly embraced American doctrine for fighting in a new way: AirLand Battle. Air power on the battlefield promised shorter, deeper and more devastating effects, shifting the relationship with reserves and resupply to one of speed and precision.[14]

The coincident understanding of the reach of Soviet effects into the British homeland forced a hardening of infrastructure and society. Defence spending, capabilities and ways of fighting became subjects of national debate – along with Soviet interference in British society through espionage, deception, subterfuge and sabotage.[15]

The Expeditionary Era

The end of the Cold War left the British in a rather unusual position. A highly capable military accustomed to long deployments overseas, and with an interventionist mindset, was now left without a key mission and unable to articulate compelling security concerns in the absence of an ideological competitor.

The emerging era of liberal internationalism was reflected in leaders such as prime ministers John Major and Tony Blair. War to liberate Kuwait in 1990–91 was followed by successful military interventions in Northern Iraq, the former Yugoslavia and Sierra Leone, in which British forces played key roles. British defence policy upheld these types of intervention, returning the UK to an expeditionary military doctrine similar to that of the pre-1914 era. The economic successes of the UK in reaping the benefits of post-Cold War optimism and a downsized military enabled

---

13 Stephen Badsey, Robin Havers and Mark Grove, *The Falklands Conflict Twenty Years on: Lessons for the Future* (London: Psychology Press, 2005).

14 Richard Lock-Pullan, 'How to Rethink War: Conceptual Innovation and AirLand Battle Doctrine', *Journal of Strategic Studies* (Vol. 28, No. 4, 2007), pp. 679–702.

15 Graham Stewart, *Bang!: A History of Britain in the 1980s* (London: Atlantic Books, 2013).

large-scale privatisation of infrastructure and a rebalancing of British debt held overseas.[16] Military activity was based on largely discretionary missions based on a moral obligation, perhaps best articulated in Tony Blair's Chicago speech in 1999 on a 'doctrine of the international community'.[17]

The intellectual relationship between the British military and technology, and thus industry, continued to direct force design towards highly technologically sophisticated platforms – albeit at much greater financial cost. Industry evolved as well. The cost of research and development was no longer underwritten by a single government, leading to a requirement for shared international development strategies, shared ownership, shared basing, and financial sector and defence business partnerships. The key political choices for the military in the post-Cold War era appeared to crystallise as being between more and cheap, or fewer and expensive. Despite that, the British military managed to maintain a balanced force, one capable of operations across the full spectrum of military conflict.

From 1999 to 2010, UK foreign and defence policy clearly articulated a requirement for such a force, and successive governments used British forces in Kosovo, Sierra Leone, Afghanistan and Iraq. But the focus on expeditionary operations and liberal interventions distracted from the re-emergence of Russia as a strategic competitor. As Secretary of State for Defence Gavin Williamson said in evidence to the House of Commons Defence Select Committee in February 2018:

> I think the world got caught napping, in terms of the rise of those state-based threats. We emerged from the Cold War with the belief that things were going to get better and better. You had one superpower that strode across the world, and you didn't really have any challenge to that. We are seeing that change quite dramatically. You are seeing the increasing assertiveness of Russia. You are seeing the fact that there has been a tenfold increase in the amount of submarine activity in the North Atlantic on behalf of the Russians.[18]

In essence, British politicians and military leaders were caught off guard, believing that future threats would stem predominantly from non-state

---

16 Adrian Johnson (ed.), *Wars in Peace* (London: RUSI, 2014).

17 Lawrence Freedman, 'Force and the International Community: Blair's Chicago Speech and the Criteria for Intervention', *International Relations* (Vol. 31, No. 2, 2017), pp. 107–24.

18 House of Commons, Defence Committee, 'Oral Evidence: Departmental Priorities', HC 814 (Q7), 21 February 2018, <http://data.parliament.uk/writtenevidence/committeeevidence.svc/evidencedocument/defence-committee/departmental-priorites/oral/78795.pdf>, accessed 13 July 2018.

actors and smaller states with relatively less-capable militaries. This to a large extent missed evolutions in combat in other parts of the world, where adversaries were adopting a doctrine of intervention and conflict designed to overcome Western enemies through distraction and dislocation by manoeuvre rather than meeting engagement and decisive battle. The UK Ministry of Defence's (MoD) expeditionary doctrine missed the changing the nature of the competition: it considered that technological innovation would suffice to offset any foreseeable adversary's military capability. This has not proved to be accurate.[19]

UK defence policy finally recognised the requirement to reprioritise security concerns after the 2015 Strategic Defence and Security Review. The High North, the North Atlantic and the Baltic have emerged as clear security priorities for the UK, albeit that military deployments and actions started earlier. It is certainly possible that new policies in 2018 will identify those geographic areas as vital national interests, underpinned by the deployment of battlegroups to the Baltic States and Eastern Europe under the Enhanced Forward Presence (EFP) mandate.

The Northern Group and the UK Joint Expeditionary Force

In 2010 Liam Fox, then UK secretary of state for defence, instigated a cooperative partnership between the Nordic countries and the UK, later expanding membership to include the Baltic States, Germany, the Netherlands and Poland. In launching the new organisation, Fox said:

> We cannot forget that geographically the United Kingdom is a northern European country. Let me be clear, this is not about carving out spheres of influence; this is about working together on mutual interests. For too long Britain has looked in every direction except its own backyard. The goal here is to deepen bilateral and multilateral relationships with key regional partners, recognising and respecting sovereignty, but also recognising that today's world is one of necessary partnership not optional isolation. In this multipolar world, we need more and different levers to act in the interests of our national and joint security. Therefore, we want to create a new and wider framework that makes it easier for both NATO and non-NATO members to have a closer relationship in the region.[20]

[19] Peter Roberts, 'Designing Conceptual Failure in Warfare: The Misguided Oath of the West', *RUSI Journal* (Vol. 162, No. 1, February/March 2017), pp. 14–23.

[20] Ministry of Defence (MoD), 'Defence Secretary Launches New Forum of Northern European Countries', 10 November 2010, <https://www.gov.uk/government/news/defence-secretary-launches-new-forum-of-northern-european-countries>, accessed 5 February 2018.

The Northern Group was not envisaged as an alternative to NATO, but did include two non-NATO states: Sweden and Finland. The meetings and forums were not specifically military in nature but focused on defence and security matters and interests. The continued close cooperation among members of this group drew interest and concern from Russian commentators. Already by 2011, the Russian media was expressing fear that the group would become the 'Arctic branch of NATO', designed to ease accession of Finland and Sweden into the Alliance.[21]

In 2014, then UK Secretary of Defence Michael Fallon extolled the utility of the partnership, stating that '[T]he Northern Group provides a key platform to help shape and deliver Europe's and NATO's response to the security implications of Russia's indefensible actions in Ukraine and whose incursions of European air and sea space have increased'.[22] Such comments continued to worry Russia.[23]

The UK remains concerned about Russia's newly assertive policy in northern Europe, viewing the region as one in which Russia is testing NATO resolve, actions and responses to provocations placed below the threshold that could trigger an Article 5 response. Diplomatic and economic responses have not proved as effective as hoped, and the EU does not appear to be an institution able to provide security guarantees to non-NATO members. Nor has NATO been able to leverage the sophisticated military capabilities that Nordic non-NATO member states can provide.

Until recently, NATO itself has appeared divided and unable to respond coherently to Russian activity, either in Northern Europe or in Ukraine. Many Alliance members with Mediterranean borders appear more concerned about mass migration than about countering Russian influence throughout the continent. This has split the Alliance into factions: those who want NATO to prioritise terrorism and migration, and those who see Russia as the clearest threat. This aspect of Alliance politics, from the British perspective at least, could not come at a worse moment. A more outspoken US administration is demanding a more effective and efficient defence partnership and apparently does not view NATO as responding with the desired agility and flexibility.

---

21 Sergei Balmasov, 'Arctic NATO to Watch the Russians', *Pravda*, 10 January 2011.

22 MoD, 'Defence Secretary Meets with Nordic-Baltic Defence Ministers', 12 November 2014, <https://www.gov.uk/government/news/defence-secretary-meets-with-nordic-baltic-defence-ministers>, accessed 13 July 2018.

23 Leonid Nersisyan, '"Severy kulak" SShA protiv Rossii: ugroza Kaliningradu i yadernim silam' ['"Northern First" The USA versus Russia: The Threat to Kaliningrad and Nuclear Powers'], <https://regnum.ru/news/polit/1913924.html>, accessed 5 February 2018.

The Northern Group has become a symbol of the potential of what willing NATO members can achieve. As such, the group has become a testing ground for a new transatlantic defence partnership that might rely on NATO as a final guarantor of security, but focuses more strongly on its own military development plan and responses. Discussions at the meeting of Northern Group defence ministers in 2017 highlighted the improved Russian military capability stationed in Kaliningrad, including new missile systems. Critically, that meeting included US Defense Secretary James Mattis.[24]

To the UK, the Northern Group appears likely to become one of the foremost defence cooperation forums for serious and genuine discussions about European security after it leaves the EU. It provides a clear structure for non-NATO states to build transatlantic security ties without engaging in the bureaucratic complexities of pursuing full NATO membership – a move that would likely raise even greater Russian concern.

Yet the Northern Group is not simply another talking shop. The member states' commitment to cooperative defence policy was supported by the creation of the JEF, a concept launched at NATO's Wales Summit in 2014, with national leaders signing a letter of intent on 5 September in Cardiff. General Sir David Richards outlined the concept at a RUSI meeting thus:

> With the capability to 'punch' hard and not be a logistical or tactical drag on a coalition, we will be especially welcomed by our friends and feared by our enemies ... [The] JEF will be capable of projecting power with global effect and influence. Nowhere is more important to us than our friends in the Middle East and Gulf and in line with clear political intent we would expect, with other initiatives, for JEF elements to spend more time reassuring and deterring in that region.[25]

The concept envisaged a group of high-readiness forces from member states, able to respond quickly to events anywhere in the world alongside like-minded states or on behalf of international organisations (such as the UN or NATO). Critically, the group was designed to be self-sufficient, and therefore not to be a drain on the resources of others (a critique often applied to NATO members that are unable or unwilling to meet their own

---

[24] *Reuters*, 'Nordic States Step Up Defence Cooperation Because of Russia Worries', 6 November 2017.

[25] MoD, 'Speech by General Sir David Richards, Chief of the Defence Staff', 17 December 2012, <https://www.gov.uk/government/speeches/chief-of-the-defence-staff-general-sir-david-richards-speech-to-the-royal-united-services-institute-rusi-17-december-2012>, accessed 4 February 2018.

needs for strategic mobility and resupply).[26] In many ways it might well evolve into a semi-independent organisation: perhaps even a Permanent Structured Cooperation-style coalition within NATO, which would allow for action by the JEF under a NATO mandate without the detailed participation by all 29 members in decision-making after a mandate has been granted.[27]

Ambition, Capability, Policy and Doctrine

While the relationship between continental Europe and the UK continues to evolve, NATO remains the constant factor: a cornerstone of British defence and security. No defence review or policy statement since 1956 has failed to acknowledge that reality. Yet it is also notable that UK defence policy statements since 2010 have placed greater weight on evidence and lessons from recent operations than on those from wider history. This selectivity creates an undercurrent in the narrative regarding the inadequacies and failures of EU security missions, and the lack of – but need for – dependable allies.

The challenge for the UK is to balance the need for presence and activity in Europe to deter Russia on the one hand and a post-Brexit political desire to be active on the world stage in order to drive a 'Global Britain' agenda on the other. Currently, the UK has neither the platforms, the doctrine, nor the funding to properly resource both these missions, as well as maintaining other existing defence commitments. Clear, unambiguous prioritisation is needed.

It might appear that a clearer British government policy has emerged, shifting distinctly towards security concerns associated with Russia. According to the political narrative at least, Moscow is challenging geographically based presumptions of safety: as a result, the UK is focusing resources, leadership and activity on the High North, the North Atlantic and the Baltic. The UK is taking an aggressive approach to Russia and the British political intent to meet aggression with deployed forces remains high, notably with continuing support for Baltic Air Policing

---

26 Håkon Lunde Saxi, 'British and German Initiatives for Defence Cooperation: The Joint Expeditionary Force and the Framework Nations Concept', *Defence Studies* (Vol. 17, No. 2, 2017).

27 The EU established a Permanent Structured Cooperation (PESCO) framework to enable security activity by some (not all) member states under the EU banner, without the presence (or agreement) of 25 member states into each specific part of planning or activity undertaken under that specific framework. See European Union External Action Service, 'Permanent Structured Cooperation (PESCO) – Factsheet', 28 June 2018, <https://eeas.europa.eu/headquarters/headquarters-Homepage/34226/permanent-structured-cooperation-pesco-factsheet_en>, accessed 13 July 2018.

missions by the RAF and NATO EFP deployments by the British Army. Yet the high-profile deployments to East Asia by scarce Royal Navy assets tells another story.

Matching resources to both ambitions – deterrence of Russia and global military presence – is likely to incur a prohibitive cost, and the military capabilities for each mission are different. The platforms and capabilities required to address the Russian threat are not those necessarily best suited for global power projection: aircraft carriers and exquisite technology may not be the best tools for deterring and countering Russian indirect confrontation and under-the-threshold warfare (the success of which appears to be centred more on political will than military hardware) but are more suitable for influence operations in East Asia. It would seem that choices are required.

Yet the UK defence establishment is not historically very good at taking difficult decisions over force design, specifically when this involves radical change. The more pragmatic – and therefore likely – course of action for the UK will be to delicately balance resources between East Asian and High North deployments. Naturally, a depleted force structure means that other commitments will have to be curtailed, whether this means deployments in continental Europe (perhaps with implications for the UK EFP missions in Estonia and eastern Europe, or Baltic Air Policing missions), EU missions (like counter-migration and counter-piracy operations in the Mediterranean Sea and Gulf of Aden), or reduced ambition in the Middle East. Accompanying this, the UK will need to change its doctrine from an emphasis on global power projection to one that balances the security of British vital national interests closer to home.

In the longer term, the continued linear evolution of military capability is simply not economically viable. The UK armed forces seem constantly in a position of reacting to Russia's latest threat platforms and capabilities, where the countermeasure is more expensive than the threat and slows operational pace and tempo. Changing this dynamic is critical to promoting a lasting regional security framework with Russia by breaking the current reliance on high technology and low political will to beat asymmetric and ambiguous activities specifically designed to bypass orthodox force structures. The forward-thinking elements of the UK MoD may understand this, but the political will (and military leadership) to undertake a true transformative change, one that would take more than a decade to achieve, has been largely absent.

The UK National Security Capability Review (NSCR), published in March 2018, pursues this balance but provides no solutions. The UK will adopt a 'modern' deterrence posture as policy and will increasingly look to Nordic states to add resilience to national defence and security arrangements. The hardening of critical national infrastructure to repel all types of attacks from Russia (kinetic or non-kinetic) and preparation for degraded network connectivity between levels of government or the disruption of business as usual appear to be increasingly prioritised, acknowledging a Russian desire to disrupt, distract and undermine NATO members. The coherence with US and French national security policies is stark. It is less clear that alignment with wider NATO policy exists – at least as was apparent in the run-up to the 2018 NATO Brussels Summit.

The NSCR makes its commitment to NATO clear, and Alliance solidarity over the nerve-agent attacks in Salisbury in March 2018 confounded many in the UK who had maligned the organisation. But underpinning the policy there is a distinct perception within the British military establishment that other European NATO members are reluctant to fulfil their own obligations for security and military spending. Many continental militaries operate with outdated equipment, are held at low readiness, and lack the political will (and fighting spirit) to engage with challenges to regional security. This lack of commitment makes such states unreliable allies and partners, a situation that resonates with British historical experience in Suez, the Falkland Islands, Iraq and Afghanistan. To a British mindset, operating with a group of like-minded states that are willing to focus on security issues and demonstrate resolve is the most attractive option. The Northern Group, therefore, seems more appealing than NATO as a whole for actual military operations in terms of specific deterrence against Russia and as a group of active partners.

Alongside this, the missions to which UK politicians accord highest priority seem to indicate a sharp contrast to UK military doctrine. Deterring Russia, not the UK's own global power projection, appears to be the chief task for the MoD – albeit balancing actions that add international credibility (such as deployments to East Asia to support sanctions against North Korea). An expeditionary approach (the concept that a state should conduct interventions at distant locations to mitigate threats closer to home) is ill-suited to the new core mission and is clearly at odds with higher-profile military deployments and the government's core security concerns. The UK is increasingly looking north – and east.

Conclusion

Within Europe, the UK is increasingly looking north to work with trusted and like-minded states, and the Northern Group and JEF mechanisms offer the greatest potential. This could be construed as part of the NATO 360-degree approach, where member states take extra responsibility in their own area. But these organisations are not recreating NATO in miniature, and not all Northern Group countries are willing to match political rhetoric with the spending such talk demands. It is likely, therefore, that the JEF has a greater chance of success because of its focus and momentum. The Russian threat has certainly given all those states involved a common sense of purpose, and the leadership provided by the UK has been welcomed (as well as the implicit connectivity to the US via the special relationship).

The Northern Group and JEF are clearly the UK's mechanisms of choice for its European mission: they have proven to be an effective way of harnessing high-readiness capability from a group of states willing and able to commit to real military activity – unlike NATO more broadly, or indeed any of the various EU structures. Formalising the JEF capability within NATO structures might represent the next logical step in delivering a meaningful and credible deterrence posture against Russia.

V. DEFENCE AND SECURITY IN NORTHERN EUROPE: A GERMAN PERSPECTIVE

KARL-HEINZ KAMP

In recent years, NATO has been confronted with a number of political and military game-changers that have demanded the most fundamental adjustment of its role and self-image since the end of the Cold War. Three developments are particularly striking.

First, in 2014, Moscow shattered the European peace by using military force to aggressively assert its great-power ambitions. Russia's illegal annexation of Crimea and its support for the rebels in Eastern Ukraine have forced NATO back into the world of Article 5, where the Alliance must back up its commitments with credible military forces.

Second, at the same time, upheaval in the Middle East and North Africa has escalated into sustained violence by state and non-state actors. Countless groups, including Islamists – supported by various regional and external powers – are fighting each other with the utmost brutality. This has led to an export of religious violence beyond these regions and in 2015 sparked a huge flood of refugees into Europe, especially into economically strong EU states such as Germany. Never before have European societies been so directly and visibly affected by destabilising developments far from their national borders.

Third, US President Donald Trump has already fundamentally altered the basics of transatlantic security relations and thereby affected the foundations of NATO. Through inexperience in foreign affairs, reliance on misleading information, and inconsistent reasoning, he has profoundly undermined the US as a moral authority and leader of the West – in other words, of the international community of liberal democracies. Moreover, he has weakened the US's traditional role as the 'benign hegemon' within

NATO by linking US security commitments to the financial contributions of its allies. This violates a core principle of deterrence, according to which commitments made by the leading power must be seen as unconditional – by both the allies and any potential aggressor.

NATO has adjusted quite successfully to the new requirements of the Article 5 world by taking decisive action in response – perhaps more firmly and effectively than Russian President Vladimir Putin had expected. The Alliance has deployed multinational combat forces – the Enhanced Forward Presence (EFP) – in Eastern Europe, significantly increased the number of military exercises it conducts, amended military contingency plans, and is making a significant effort to improve military logistics to facilitate moving forces east in the event of a crisis.

On the downside, differing threat perceptions and strategic cultures – again due to geographical and historical factors – have led to different priorities within the Alliance and to a compartmentalised debate on NATO's tasks and requirements. 'Easterners' and 'southerners' have vigorously argued about where NATO should focus its attention and resources. The three Baltic States, Poland, and most other Eastern European members tend to concentrate on potential threats posed by Russia, requesting that NATO dedicate most of its efforts to deploying a credible defence against Russian aggression. However, they often ignore the fact that, unlike in the Cold War, when the Soviet Union potentially threatened the very survival of almost all NATO members, some allies today perceive Russia's activities as a concern, but not necessarily an existential threat.

This holds particularly true for southern allies such as Italy and Spain, who point to the threats emerging from south of the Mediterranean Sea and encourage NATO to focus on terrorism, Islamist violence and refugees. However, they face the problem of clearly expressing what NATO could actually do to address their security concerns. Whereas the danger posed by Russia is a direct and immediate one (at least for Northern and Eastern Europe), which can be tackled using appropriate and mostly military means, the threats from the south are of a more socioeconomic nature, against which a primarily military alliance such as NATO can do very little with the instruments it has available.

A further group in the debate consists of the Nordic states, which also focus on the Russian threat from the East but insist that NATO should not neglect what was once called the 'Northern Flank'. Besides the somewhat obvious argument that NATO stands for *North Atlantic* Treaty Organisation, Norway in particular has pointed out that a military confrontation with Russia may not occur only in the Baltic region or in the so-called Suwalki Gap along the Polish–Lithuanian border, but also include the North Atlantic. This region is of strategic as well as economic importance given the potential exploitation of its natural resources and commercial shipping routes. NATO therefore not only needs to guarantee an EFP in Eastern Europe, but must also prepare its forces to fight under the severe climatic conditions of Northern Europe.

Germany's New Security Policy

In 2014 there was a turning point for Germany's foreign and security policy and its role in the North Atlantic Alliance. In February 2014, at the Munich Security Conference, then President Joachim Gauck, Foreign Minister Frank-Walter Steinmeier and Defence Minister Ursula von der Leyen publicly promised greater German engagement in countering international crises and conflicts.[1] The domestic and international reactions to this surprising promise ranged from benign scepticism to outright dismissal. The majority of Germans disagreed with the idea; public opposition was visible in newspapers and on television, with commentators warning of a 'militarisation' of German foreign policy. Germany's NATO and EU allies could hardly believe that the country would suddenly adopt a fundamentally changed approach to foreign policy. Russia had not yet annexed the Crimean Peninsula and the Middle East had not yet reached its current state of instability. Why should the announcements made in Munich signify more than vague intentions often expressed on such occasions?

It is worth noting, however, that the political signal sent in Munich was not unexpected. In fact, the origins of this policy shift go back to the Libya crisis in 2011. Not only had Germany refused to participate in the NATO operation against Libya, but the German government had also decided – in opposition to its Western allies – to abstain on the UN Security Council resolution authorising military action in Libya. Germany found itself in the company of Russia, China and Brazil, thereby also delivering a snub to its closest friends and partners. The price it paid for this lack of Alliance solidarity was painful. For many months, Germany lost much of its influence on developments within NATO and was also excluded from inner-circle debates. Even close EU partners such as France kept their distance from Germany for a considerable time. As a result, when Angela Merkel was elected to her

1 Bundespraesident (Office of the German President), 'Germany's Role in the World: Reflections on Responsibility, Norms and Alliances', speech by Federal President Joachim Gauck at the opening of the 2014 Munich Security Conference, 31 January 2014, <http://www.bundespraesident.de/SharedDocs/Downloads/DE/Reden/2014/01/140131-Muenchner-Sicherheitskonferenz-Englisch.pdf?__blob=publicationFile>, accessed 18 July 2018.

third term as chancellor in 2013, a tacit consensus had emerged within the new coalition of Social Democrats and Conservatives that this disaster should never be repeated.

Arguably, the three Munich speeches alone may not in themselves have sufficed to change Germany's course in foreign policy. Instead, it took a political catalyst in the shape of Russia's revanchist ambitions to achieve the shift.

Germany rapidly responded to the new challenges NATO was facing in the Article 5 world. Politically, it adopted a clear anti-Russian stance, for instance by strongly supporting EU sanctions in response to Moscow's aggression. Militarily, Berlin committed itself to strengthening NATO deterrence in Eastern Europe and becoming a leading element of the EFP in Lithuania. It deployed forces to the east and conducted more frequent military exercises. Later, in 2018, Germany successfully applied to host and run a NATO logistic command, the Joint Support and Enabling Command (JSEC) – a decision that followed from the insight that German territory would be the hub for any NATO force movements to the east in the event of a crisis. Moreover, through concrete military steps, such as taking the lead on the JSEC, Berlin could counter the Trump administration's criticism of not spending enough on defence.

Furthermore, by providing lethal weapons to the Kurdish Peshmerga fighters in Iraq, Germany even broke its historic taboo on delivering arms to an ongoing military conflict. All this resulted in increased spending and investments in defence. In the period from 2014 to 2018, Germany's parliament, which must authorise all military purchases, approved a total of €32 billion for military equipment; in the preceding four years, the country's military purchases had amounted to only €6 billion.

At the same time, the extent to which the German Bundeswehr had been neglected over the past decades became apparent. Germany, like many other European allies, had benefited from the peace dividend since the fall of the Berlin Wall by severely cutting back its defence spending. Beginning in 2001, Germany became engaged in a dangerous combat operation in Afghanistan that required the purchase of specialised military equipment, for instance, to enable counterinsurgency operations. Meanwhile, the country reduced its defence spending even further – although Germany contributed the third-largest number of troops to NATO operations in Afghanistan. The cuts resulted in insufficient maintenance and replacement of weapons and materiel, which in turn led to outdated equipment and hollowed-out military structures. This explains why Germany's armed forces must still cope with non-operational tanks, damaged submarines in dry dock, a shortage of helicopter parts, and a lack of modern aircraft – despite the strategic turnaround in defence spending that Berlin initiated in 2014.[2]

Even critics who acknowledge the government's efforts have complained that Berlin is not implementing the new policy of stronger military engagement more rigorously, particularly because economic conditions seem favourable at the moment. The questions they ask include: Why is it so difficult for Berlin even to come close to NATO's target of 2 per cent of GDP on defence spending, given that the country's economic performance is better than that of most other NATO and EU countries? Why is there insufficient political leadership to shift public opinion towards accepting larger defence budgets if the sorry state of the Bundeswehr seems so obvious?

The main reason is that, because of its history, Germany has a different relationship with its military than countries such as France or the UK. Germans still do not consider armed forces an instrument to be used in state affairs, and they are also not a source of national pride. Changing this aspect of the German nation's psyche, at least in part, will take time and will almost certainly occur only in very small steps. Nevertheless, it is also worth mentioning that the evolution towards a more realistic approach to military requirements already started some time ago. During the first Gulf War in 1991, when the US discussed the situation in Kuwait with its allies, white sheets with the slogan 'No Blood for Oil' hung from many windows in Germany. In 1999 – eight years later – Germany joined NATO's combat mission in Kosovo, even though that mission was not mandated by the UN Security Council. From 2001, Germany suffered casualties in Afghanistan, yet remained fully committed in the campaign. Today, the German public has become used to talking about 'veterans', 'war casualties' and 'medals for bravery', although these terms were considered toxic just a few years ago. The government even published a white paper in 2016 that cited prosperity, free trade and access to raw materials as vital German interests;[3] yet only six years earlier, in 2010, President Horst Köhler had to resign after making a similar statement during a public speech.

Germany and its Northern Neighbours

In light of these realities, Germany is now struggling to respond to a number of contradictory and controversial requirements. Given its role and

[2] For more details, see Christopher Woody, 'Germany's Military Falling Behind, and the US is Putting it on Notice', *Business Insider*, 3 February 2018.

[3] German Federal Government, 'White Paper 2016: On German Security Policy and the Future of the Bundeswehr', June 2016, <https://issat.dcaf.ch/download/111704/2027268/2016%20White%20Paper.pdf>, accessed 18 July 2018.

relevance within NATO, Germany is trying to mediate between various groups – easterners, southerners and northerners. It fully understands that, in the current situation in Europe and further afield, a holistic perspective is necessary to deal with security challenges. At the same time, the military capabilities of its armed forces remain limited and clearly inadequate for one of the leading countries in NATO and the EU. The government has initiated fundamental changes with respect to military deployments in Eastern Europe and crisis-management operations in the Middle East and Northern Africa, but it will take a long time before any results are realised, and the Bundeswehr will constantly have to defend its increased budgets against the traditional scepticism towards the military.

This situation has drawn criticism from almost all sides. Even if NATO in general very much welcomes Germany's involvement in re-establishing a credible military deterrence in Eastern Europe, individual members still complain about the Bundeswehr's lack of capability to rapidly move combat-ready forces to the east in the event of a crisis.[4] Its southern allies want Germany to show greater commitment in the Middle East, and France in particular is demanding a greater German presence in Africa. Even the northern countries occasionally complain that an export-oriented country such as Germany does not – as they see it – show more support for bringing the North Atlantic and the Greenland–Iceland–UK Gap back onto NATO's agenda. On top of all this, the opposition parties in Germany can still score points by lamenting about the 'militarisation' of security policy, as if Russian President Vladimir Putin's ambitions or Islamist violence could be countered merely through diplomacy, arms control and political dialogue.

To a large extent, Germany attempts to overcome existing shortcomings through close cooperation with others. The close interaction planned with the UK, as described in the UK's 2015 Strategic Defence and Security Review, was stalled by Brexit and the ongoing withdrawal negotiations. Germany did establish an exceptional degree of cooperation with the Netherlands, with the two countries linking their land and naval forces and integrating each other's units into their own military structures. With respect to the Nordic countries, Germany is trying to achieve the seemingly impossible by reconciling contradictory requirements, primarily through close bilateral relations. However, the depth and intensity of these relations vary. At the same time, Germany is following its traditional cautious strategic approach by passively supporting the multilateral

---

[4] Michael Shurkin, *The Abilities of the British, French, and German Armies to Generate and Sustain Armored Brigades in the Baltics* (Santa Monica, CA: RAND Corporation, 2017).

strategy of the Arctic Council on the basis of its observer status in that institution.

Sweden

Germany cooperates very closely with Sweden, which has also fundamentally reassessed its security policy since 2014, even reintroducing conscription – a step currently not being discussed seriously in Germany. Representatives of both countries have stated that Swedish–German cooperation enhances security in Europe in general, and in the Baltic Sea region in particular. Sweden considers Germany as one of its closest partners, along with Finland. The Ghent Initiative of November 2010, in which both countries suggested stronger pooling and sharing of their military capabilities, is an example of this partnership.[5] In June 2017, the defence ministers of the two countries signed a letter of intent (replacing a document signed in May 2010) to further strengthen cooperation. Joint activities are to include a pooling of mine-sweeping capabilities, military education, helicopter pilot training, and medical support to missions. Sweden in particular supports the German Framework Nation Concept (FNC) by contributing niche capabilities such as the maritime transport of helicopters and military intelligence in the context of Germany as lead nation. Good relations were sustained during some minor commercial tensions over the Swedish shipyard Kockums, which was temporarily owned by the German company ThyssenKrupp Marine Systems but has since been repurchased by the Saab Group.

Another dimension of bilateral relations includes multinational missions in countries such as Afghanistan (*Resolute Support*) and Mali (MINUSMA), where Sweden provides C-130 transport aircraft. Sweden has shown particular interest in exercises with the German Bundeswehr in preparation for such missions.

Finland

Finland is another of Germany's major partners. Unlike Sweden, which wants close ties with NATO but firmly rejects any discussion of membership, Finland has responded to Russia's growing assertiveness by reopening its debate about NATO membership. Helsinki therefore supports Germany's tough position on upholding the EU sanctions against

---

5 See, for instance, 'Pooling and Sharing, German-Swedish Initiative', November 2010, the *Food for Thought* paper drafted by the two countries, <http://www.europarl.europa.eu/meetdocs/2009_2014/documents/sede/dv/sede260511deseinitiative_/sede260511deseinitiative_en.pdf>, accessed 6 April 2018.

Russia, even if this results in measurable costs to the Finnish economy. At the same time, Finland also understands that – due to geographic proximity – it has little choice but to constructively deal with Russia.

Bilateral relations between Finland and Germany are close, based on trust. This is reflected in the Letter of Intent of June 2017, which provides for closer cooperation, as well as in the regular talks between the military staffs of both countries every eighteen months. Germany contributes financially to the Finnish Centre of Excellence on Hybrid Warfare and greatly appreciates Finland's military contributions in Afghanistan and during the training mission in Iraq. Like Sweden, Finland has a strong interest in joint military exercises and in Germany's role as a military framework nation.

Norway

Germany's relations with Norway are excellent, although shaped by different conditions than with Sweden and Finland, primarily based on NATO membership rather than EU.

Germany and Norway established a framework for more intensive cooperation with a bilateral declaration of intent signed in Bodø in September 2011. The most visible result of this declaration was the signing of a Memorandum of Understanding on Naval Defence Material Cooperation in June 2017. The memorandum covers five different projects: submarine cooperation; missile cooperation; navy-to-navy contacts; defence industrial cooperation; and research-and-development cooperation. In late 2017, Germany offered further cooperation in battle-tank development. The German coalition agreement of March 2018 lists Norway as one of three countries (along with France and the Netherlands) with which Germany wants to extend its defence cooperation.[6] In the context of NATO, Norway supports the German EFP battalion with a tank company, and also has a strong interest in Germany acting as a military framework nation. In 2019, Germany, Norway and the Netherlands will again spearhead the NATO Response Force.

However, despite close bilateral relations, there is a need for greater agreement on conceptual issues. While Germany supports Norway's advocacy of a stronger NATO presence in the North Atlantic and the establishment of a new regional command, it is reluctant to increase the Bundeswehr's presence in this region substantially. Rather than deploy a

6 Koalitionsvertrag zwischen CDU, CSU und SPD, 'Ein neuer Aufbruch für Europa. Eine neue Dynamik für Deutschland. Ein neuer Zusammenhalt für unser Land', p. 144, <https://www.bundesregierung.de/Content/DE/_Anlagen/2018/03/2018-03-14-koalitionsvertrag.pdf;jsessionid=03C5473377E0378E6F2159C2F96F8CB1.s5t1?__blob=publicationFile&v=5>, accessed 18 July 2018.

larger naval force to the North Atlantic or commit to specific bilateral reinforcement plans for land forces, Germany sees participation in large-scale exercises such as *Trident Juncture 2018* as its contribution to security and stability in this region. This stems from divergent threat perceptions and the need for prioritisation of limited capabilities.

Denmark

Given Greenland's geographic proximity to the Arctic, Denmark is the only EU member that is also a member of the Arctic Five (along with Russia, Canada, the US, and Norway). It therefore has particular relevance for Germany. As in Norway, political developments in Washington and London prompted a domestic debate in Denmark on whether the country should maintain its traditional transatlantic orientation, or whether it should reverse its scepticism towards EU military capabilities.

Denmark has close military ties with US, UK and French armed forces, and ranks Germany behind these countries, although it is still considered a privileged partner. This stems in part from concerns about Germany's policy of strict parliamentary control over the armed forces. Denmark fears this principle could lead to unduly long decision-making processes and affect the combat readiness of the Bundeswehr. Denmark is a framework nation in the Multinational Corps Northeast, together with Poland and Germany. These countries expressed some irritation in 2017 when Denmark stated it was no longer prepared to pay its one-third share of the overall costs, but this issue has since been resolved.

The Future of Germany's Engagement in the North

Germany has fulfilled its 2014 pledge to make a greater contribution to strengthening NATO's deterrence in Eastern Europe. In addition, it has intensified cooperation with its northern neighbours to exploit military synergies and achieve an overall improvement in Europe's defence capabilities. It remains to be seen whether this effort was sufficient or whether it merely reflected the upper limit of what Berlin could achieve in view of the German public's traditional scepticism towards the military. Moreover, the interesting question remains as to how Germany's security and defence policy will evolve in the coming years and to what degree Germany will be willing and able to place a stronger emphasis on the northern security dimension. Given the current political situation, it is possible to put forward a few speculative assumptions.

First, despite populist movements on the right and left, German governments are likely to remain dominated by moderate parties. Meanwhile, the 2018 grand coalition of Social Democrats and conservatives is likely to continue adjusting Germany's security and defence policy to meet the requirements of the Article 5 world. That prominent voices often strongly reject NATO's target of spending 2 per cent of GDP on defence is due more to the domestic debate in Germany than to a fundamental unwillingness to increase investment in the country's underfunded armed forces. Ministry of Defence medium-term plans therefore propose a spending increase of €15 billion in the period 2019–22. The new total would amount to approximately 1.5 per cent of GDP.

According to military planners, this is already the maximum the German armed forces can realistically absorb, given lengthy military procurement processes and the difficulty of recruiting additional personnel for the armed forces in a booming economy. On the other hand, the Social Democrat (and traditionally anti-defence spending) coalition partner has become increasingly weak politically. Since the politically stronger Christian Democrats would risk the coalition if support for the Social Democrats fell below a certain proportion of the electorate, Chancellor Angela Merkel could be forced to slow the intended rise of the defence budget. The coming years will show how Germany manages to steer between domestic necessities and allied pressure.

Second, Germany's movement towards greater international responsibility as well as the need to explain strategic necessities to an – at least partially – sceptical public will intensify in the coming years. A number of inconvenient questions will inevitably resurface during this period after being ignored for a long time. One of these questions, which will also affect cooperation with northern neighbours, concerns arms exports. Germany has traditionally adopted a much more restrictive approach on exporting military goods than most of its European allies, particularly France. Even so, there is still public criticism that Germany sells weapons to other countries at all. To defuse these concerns and remove the issue from the headlines, German governments have always pointed to their long-term goal of harmonising the various export policies of individual European nations within the framework of a common EU arms-export policy. At the same time, they have declared that such a common approach should not be more lenient than Germany's strict national guidelines. This question is relevant not only to domestic or economic issues, but also to EU Permanent Structured Cooperation (PESCO) or other bilateral and trilateral arrangements. If Germany does not clarify its position on arms exports, close industrial cooperation and joint development will be unlikely.

Given that the current government remains deeply committed to both reviving Franco–German defence cooperation and making a stronger effort on the EU Common Security and Defence Policy (CSDP), it will not be long before the export issue is back on the domestic agenda. The government would be forced to admit that its policy of seeking a common EU approach as strict as the German national export policy in essence amounts to a contradiction in terms. Decisions within the EU framework always reflect compromises between the various views of all member states and therefore – by definition – cannot be consistent with the most extreme proposal on the negotiation table. It follows that any common EU arms-export policy would be more permissive than the German policy. Therefore, instead of avoiding an unpleasant issue, the government would need to engage in a public debate about strategic, economic and institutional (CSDP) interests in arms exports on the one hand and public concerns on the other. A debate of this kind, which would arise in the context of military-industrial cooperation with northern allies, may well be painful, but it could help to broaden the general political consensus on a coherent security policy.

Third, Germany is likely to retain its continental approach, not least because of its limited resources. Ensuring security in the North Atlantic has a strong maritime dimension – and the Deutsche Marine is the smallest of the German armed forces – which helps to explain why successive governments in Berlin have so far always seen the High North primarily from an environmental or climate-related point of view rather than from a hard-security perspective; thus, Germany's 2016 white paper does not explicitly mention the northern maritime domain. This does not rule out closer cooperation with northern countries, but the strategic focus of German defence policy will likely be on Eastern Europe and a limited number of stabilisation missions south of the Mediterranean. The most urgent priority for the German armed forces currently is to build up sufficient capabilities to counter Article 5 threats in Eastern Europe.

Conclusion

Germany will undoubtedly continue to adjust and deliver military capabilities as swiftly as possible within NATO and the EU, although perhaps not as rapidly as some may expect. At the same time, its threat perceptions and defence priorities will never be as Nordic as those of Norway, for instance, or as Eastern as those of Poland and Estonia – nor will they become as Western as those of France or the UK when it comes to using military force. Given Germany's strategic position and its political and economic influence, Berlin must pursue a multidirectional policy that unites different factions in NATO, matures its domestic debate, and also provides support to the Alliance in general.

Through its FNC initiative, substantial contributions to NATO's reassurance and deterrence measures, and participation in international operations – including Afghanistan, Iraq and Mali – Germany has, over the last five years, re-established itself as one of the major security players in Europe. The countries of Northern Europe, which see Germany as a like-minded and reliable partner, appreciate this increased role and are willing to extend bilateral and multilateral cooperation with Germany in capability projects and military missions. Relying on Germany to strengthen the European pillar of the transatlantic alliance during the uncertainty provoked by Trump and Brexit could be a feasible option for most countries of the region, regardless of their affiliation with the EU and NATO. To be an anchor or framework nation, however, requires that Germany keep its promise of a more active foreign and security policy made in 2014 and its pledge of increased defence spending made at the Wales Summit.

That said, it is worth recapitulating that all European allies are confronted with a new and unexpected challenge that could alter the trajectory of European defence cooperation: the unclear course of NATO's 'benign hegemon' – the US. What began as the actions of a president whose behaviour was expected to be moderated by a group of thoughtful advisers has now apparently mushroomed into a transatlantic crisis deeper than those over nuclear missiles in the 1980s or over Iraq in 2003. It seems that President Trump is systematically destroying the basis of Alliance policies, which might even pose a fatal threat to NATO as an institution. Even assuming that the US elects a different president in 2020, a new administration is likely to regard Russia as a decreasing power and to focus on China as the primary global rival. From such a perspective, the US is likely to assess its European allies mainly according to their value as instruments for new global competition with Beijing. This attitude would shake the foundations that transatlantic relations have rested upon for the past 70 years. The new danger of NATO being undermined as the most successful security institution of modern history, combined with a crumbling EU which has so far failed to overcome its internal economic and political crises, amounts to a poisonous mix which will affect all European security relations – and not only in the North.

VI. NETHERLANDS DEFENCE AND SECURITY POLICY: COPING WITH THE 'NEW NORMAL'?

FRANS OSINGA

Defence Planning in the New Era of Certainty

Uncertainty is an overused term these days when it comes to security policy and defence planning in Europe.[1] Of course, international relations and wars are fundamentally non-linear; rapid technological change, geopolitical shifts and societal upheaval are also sources of uncertainty. The current era definitely qualifies as a time of change, with liberalism claimed to be in retreat; the West losing its dominance in international politics as well as its military superiority; waning influence of international institutions such as the EU, the UN and NATO; and Asia increasingly the most important locus of geopolitical developments. But uncertainty can also be over-emphasised. Not all risks are equal; some are closer to home than others and some threaten vital and strategic interests, whereas others may 'merely' threaten stability or economic interests.

In this respect, life for European defence planners has, regrettably, become relatively straightforward since 2014. Russia's annexation of Crimea has reduced uncertainty: in addition to preparing for interventions in the 'arc of instability', European militaries must now re-learn and re-equip to deter and potentially fight inter-state war on the European continent. Whether that certainty will translate into defence policies that will reduce security risks is still an open question. Indeed, as this chapter argues, the Netherlands is an illustrative case study that suggests this new age of certainty for defence planners offers no grounds for optimism

[1] Patrick Porter, 'Taking Uncertainty Seriously: Classical Realism and National Security', *European Journal of International Security* (Vol. 1, No. 2, 2016), pp. 239–60.

about European security. Moreover, in contrast to the defence planning context pre-2014, the consequences of inadequate planning now concern actual threats and not mere abstract risks.

Netherlands Security and Defence Policy Before 2014

From 1990 to 2014, security and defence policy development in the Netherlands – informed by both a transatlantic and European mind-set – tended to closely follow NATO and EU thinking.[2] During the years of this 'strategic pause', think tank reports and governmental security and defence white papers in the West invariably stressed uncertainty: yet European security was not fundamentally threatened. Indeed, a certain triumphalism – an attitude often associated with Francis Fukuyama's famous 'end of history' thesis – set in, assuming that, for now, the Western liberal-democratic model of ordering societies had no competitor. NATO member states now had to manage risks instead of threats.[3] Wars of choice replaced wars of necessity, as Lawrence Freedman famously quipped in the mid-1990s. National security was replaced by human security, and European security was increasingly associated with the ability to create stability in the regions around Europe. As the EU Security Strategy of 2003 asserted, Europe needed to be surrounded by a 'ring of well-governed countries'. In order to accomplish that, Europe needed to develop a proactive culture that fostered early intervention to help contain conflicts, 'manage violence', remove the sources of state fragility and failure, and create conditions that enabled the re-emergence of peaceful political processes and civil society, preferably along the model of Western societies. The NATO Strategic Concept of 2010 expressed the consensus view up to 2014: terrorism, cyber threats, refugee flows, humanitarian disasters, and failing states ranked high among the risks that NATO identified.

These views were reflected in a series of Netherlands Ministry of Defence white papers such as the Defence Priority Review (1993), the Defence White Paper (2000), the Budget Day Letter (2003), the policy letter 'Service Worldwide' (2007), and the policy letter 'The Ministry of

---

[2] For the strategic culture of the Netherlands see, for instance, Frans Osinga and Rob de Wijk, 'Innovating on a Shrinking Playing Field', in Theo Farrell, Terry Terriff and Frans Osinga (eds), *A Transformation Gap? American Innovations and European Military Change* (Palo Alto, CA: Stanford University Press, 2010).

[3] See Frans Osinga and Julian Lindley-French, 'Leading Military Organizations in the Risk Society', in Joseph Soeters et al. (eds), *Managing Military Organizations* (Abingdon: Routledge, 2010), pp. 17–28; Christopher Coker, *War in an Age of Risk* (New York, NY: Polity, 2009). For European strategic cultures, see Heiko Biehl et al. (eds), *Strategic Cultures in Europe* (Potsdam: Springer, 2013).

Defence after the Credit Crisis' (2011). The main focus of Dutch security and defence policy up to 2014 was the promotion of the rule of international law and the deployment of the armed forces in peacekeeping and peace-enforcement operations around the world. Absent a major shock, no-one suggested that missions of the future and their associated political constraints and geographical, logistical and operational challenges, or indeed future opponents, would radically differ from those of the previous two decades. Future risks to European interests, and therefore also Dutch interests, were associated with the arc of instability: that would be the future operational environment for which the Dutch military needed to prepare. Thus, defence analysts and planners proclaiming that the future was uncertain were overstating their argument.

But optimism in strategic surveys, published annually from 2010 onwards, gave way to concern that stability in global politics was decreasing. In its 2012 letter, the Adviesraad Internationale Vraagstukken (Advisory Council on International Affairs – AIV) warned that, in view of the emerging national and international security risks, further defence cutbacks were irresponsible. It further warned that:

> it is also important to realise that once military capability has been hived off, rebuilding it can take years or even decades. Today the armed forces' capacity for deployment is already limited. Additional cutbacks would have a disastrous impact on the defence organisation, as well as being in conflict with the constitutionally mandated tasks of the armed forces and the Netherlands' obligations under international agreements.[4]

Despite such ominous predictions in official advisory reports to the Cabinet, defence spending in 2012 continued its decline of the previous two decades. The alleged level of uncertainty embedded in strategic surveys undergirded the decision to apply a 'broad toolbox approach': maintaining a heterogeneous portfolio of low- and high-end capabilities was deemed prudent in light of the unpredictability of the security environment as well as the experience of the previous two decades, during which Netherlands military units had been involved not only in a variety of peacekeeping missions but also in high-intensity campaigns such as *Deliberate Force*, *Allied Force* and *Unified Protector*. The International Security Assistance Force (ISAF) in Afghanistan demonstrated that stabilisation and counterinsurgency missions also require high-end capabilities for

[4] Advisory Council on International Affairs (AIV), 'Open Letter to a New Dutch Government; The Armed Forces at Risk', 11 September 2012, p. 9, <https://aiv-advies.nl/6fs/publications/advisory-letters/open-letter-to-a-new-dutch-government-the-armed-forces-at-risk>, accessed 18 July 2018.

intelligence purposes and force protection; hence the continuous deployment of Dutch F-16s and AH-64 attack helicopters. Finally, as a relatively small country with limited military capabilities, the Netherlands recognised that maintaining expensive niche capabilities, such as air-to-air refuelling tankers, submarines and Patriot surface-to-air missile systems, all of which are scarce in NATO, offered political benefits in coalition politics. The broad toolbox approach offered a sufficient range of military capabilities which the Cabinet could choose from to contribute to the most likely set of international military missions. This logic informed the 2013 Netherlands Ministry of Defence White Paper, 'In the Interest of the Netherlands'.[5]

On the other hand, the global financial crisis; public opinion that prioritised social security, jobs and health care; and the realities of political compromise which coalition governments required, forced continuation of the Cabinet policy of 2010 – amounting to approximately €1 billion in permanent cuts. Apart from a freeze in military salaries and further closing of military facilities, this necessitated cutting the planned number of F-35s set to replace the ageing F-16s (which in 1991 numbered 211 airframes) to 37 instead of 65, scrapping the entire fleet of Leopard main battle tanks (which once numbered 935), and mothballing most of the relatively new self-propelled artillery. By 2013, the investment ratio within the defence budget had fallen sharply to just 14 per cent of the total defence budget instead of the 20 per cent deemed necessary. In 2012 the Advisory Council on International Affairs warned that the defence budget of only €7.87 billion, or 1.3 per cent of GDP, compared starkly with the level of 2.7 per cent spent in 1990. The budget also included €1.3 billion for pensions, benefits and redundancy pay, and another €372 million was spent on the Royal Military and Border Police (Koninklijke Marechaussee), most of whose tasks are unrelated to the armed forces. The AIV concluded that the defence budget cast Dutch defence efforts in a troubling light vis-à-vis the deteriorating security environment.[6] By 2015, that budget had declined to only 1.09 per cent of the Netherlands, GDP, a far cry from NATO's 2 per cent goal, and also well below the European average of 1.43 per cent.

While politically inevitable, the 2013 White Paper attracted criticism for free-riding. The shrinking defence budget was also considered incompatible with the fact that the Netherlands economy – ranked 16–17th globally in terms of GDP – is very sensitive to international developments and depends on stable trade flows and well-functioning, effective

---

[5] Netherlands Ministry of Defence, 'In the Interest of the Netherlands', <https://www.google.com/search?client=safari&rls=en&q=In+the+Interest+of+the+Netherlands&ie=UTF-8&oe=UTF-8#>, accessed 18 July 2018.

[6] AIV, 'Open Letter to a New Dutch Government; The Armed Forces at Risk', p. 6.

international institutions.[7] The views in the paper were also deemed incompatible with the deteriorating international security situation and the increasing US critique on European defence spending.[8] The AIV echoed the sobering words of the Ministry of Defence policy letter, 'The Ministry of Defence after the Credit Crisis: Reduced Armed Forces in a Turbulent World', that these cuts made it impossible to fully achieve the Netherlands' objective of building versatile and expeditionary armed forces.

The Shock of the Old: 2014

In March 2014 the relatively permissive security environment ended with the annexation of Crimea, the emergence of a revisionist Russia, the rise of Daesh (also known as the Islamic State of Iraq and Syria, ISIS), and the refugee crisis hitting European states. One year later, the AIV in its report to the Cabinet commented that 2014 had been a watershed year:[9] it marked the end of the crisis-management paradigm, which assumed that Western military power enjoyed unfettered access to the 'global commons'.

Russia's overt aggression in particular removed a substantial degree of uncertainty for European defence planners, given its assessed aim to destabilise institutions such as the EU and NATO and erode their bonds with Eastern European states. In its multi-pronged approach, termed 'hybrid warfare',[10] Russia demonstrates a sophisticated form of state influence and control, using multiple tools in a coordinated and often coercive fashion. The modernisation of Russian conventional forces has also raised concern. The combination of these capabilities translates into options to rapidly create situations on the ground that would force NATO and the EU to develop quick responses. Russia could then influence those responses by threatening nuclear escalation. NATO military capabilities may outnumber those of Russia in most categories, but these assets are scattered across Europe and NATO's deployed forces are insufficient to

---

[7] For a summary of this debate see, for instance, Ida van Veldhuizen et al., *Geopolitiek en Defensie: Pal staan voor vrijheid en veiligheid* [*Geopolitics and Defence: Stand Up for Freedom and Security*] (The Hague: Telders Stichting, 2017), pp. 103–6; Frank Bekkers et al., *De Waarde van Defensie* [*The Value of Defence*] (The Hague: The Hague Centre for Strategic Studies, September 2012).

[8] AIV, 'Open Letter to a New Dutch Government; The Armed Forces at Risk', p. 8.

[9] AIV, 'Instability Around Europe: Confrontation with a New Reality', 15 September 2015, Foreword, <https://aiv-advies.nl/85t/publications/advisory-reports/instability-around-europe-confrontation-with-a-new-reality>, accessed 18 July 2018.

[10] See, for instance, Alexander Lanoszka, 'Russian Hybrid Warfare and Extended Deterrence in Eastern Europe', *International Affairs* (Vol. 92, No. 1, 2016); for a lengthy treatment of Russian hybrid warfare from a NATO perspective, see Guillaume Lasconjerias and Jeffrey A Larsen (eds), *NATO's Response to Hybrid Threats*, Forum Paper 24 (Rome: NATO Defense College, 2015).

defend a continuous line and delay a large-scale conventional advance by a mechanised adversary such as Russia – particularly as Russian forces would have sufficient mobility to concentrate forces in time and space to substantially outnumber isolated defenders.

Russia's anti-access/area denial (A2AD) capabilities – such as electronic-warfare systems, cyber-warfare capabilities, long-range surface-to-surface missiles (SSMs), and surface-to-air missiles (SAMs) – aggravate this strategic problem. They deny NATO its traditional leading edge and undermine its preferred mode of warfare. While its long-range SSMs and artillery outrange NATO's, Russia has particularly geared its military modernisation towards negating NATO's asymmetric advantage in air power.[11] With its massed SSM and SAM capabilities, Russia can deny air space over large parts of the Balkans and Poland. It can also threaten military facilities, transport infrastructure and thus reinforcement (such as the Very High Readiness Joint Task Force – VJTF) in Eastern Europe and well into Germany. It can further deny the use of sea lines of communications. A RAND study concludes that 'NATO cannot successfully defend the territory of its most exposed members'.[12] Former US Ambassador to NATO Ivo Daalder, therefore urged recently that 'today, Russia poses a threat unlike any the US and its allies have faced since the end of the Cold War … If they fail to unite and bolster NATO's defense capabilities, Europe's future stability and security may well be imperiled'.[13]

Responding to the Certainty of the New Normal

In the 2015 letter 'Turbulent Times in Unstable Surroundings', the Netherlands government acknowledged that this new situation changed the underlying basis of existing policies.[14] It concluded:

> On both our eastern and southern borders we are faced with hybrid warfare, combining conventional, irregular and cyber tactics … The importance of defending our own and our allies' territory has

[11] Thomas R McCabe, 'The Russian Perception of the NATO Aerospace Threat', *Air and Space Power Journal* (Fall 2016), p. 65.

[12] David A Shlapak and Michael Johnson, *Reinforcing Deterrence on NATO's Eastern Flank: Wargaming the Defense of the Baltics* (Santa Monica, CA: RAND, 2016), p. 1.

[13] Ivo Daalder, 'Responding to Russia's Resurgence: Not Quiet on the Eastern Front', *Foreign Affairs* (Vol. 96, No. 6, November/December 2017), p. 38.

[14] Netherlands Ministry of Foreign Affairs, 'Turbulent Times in Unstable Surroundings', 16 January 2015, p. 5, <https://www.government.nl/documents/parliamentary-documents/2015/01/16/turbulent-times-in-unstable-surroundings>, accessed 18 July 2018.

> returned with a vengeance. Strategic relations in the Black Sea region have changed radically. The Ukraine crisis has given transatlantic cooperation … a new dimension. NATO solidarity has become even more crucial: our allies must be able to count on us, and vice versa. Within NATO, the Ukraine crisis has led to a reaffirmation of the importance of collective defence.[15]

In its 2017 report, the AIV warned that, in light of NATO's persistent capability shortfalls and its internal disagreements, the Alliance's deterrence posture was inadequate.[16] The current posture may force NATO to consider a strategy of deterrence by punishment, leaving the initiative with NATO to escalate: not an attractive option given an adversary that has declared a willingness to escalate to the use of nuclear weapons. There is no doubt therefore that academics, think tanks, advisory bodies, and defence and foreign affairs officials in the Netherlands are fully aware of and acknowledged the contours of the 'new normal'.

In response, in 2016 the Netherlands increased investments in cyber defences, committed itself to NATO's EFP initiative, and continued its commitment to the Baltic Air Policing mission. International cooperation, which has always been a key feature of Netherlands defence policy, was intensified with a new cooperation agreement between the Netherlands and Germany and with a commitment to the EU's Permanent Structured Cooperation (PESCO) initiative. The buzzwords of 'innovation' and 'adaptive force' have materialised in projects such as the Big Data Science Cell, investments in national micro-satellites, and research into the concept of a 'Netforce' – a reframing of the NATO Network Enabled Capabilities concept of the early 2000s. Intelligence services and cyber capabilities also received more emphasis.

Still, the overall budget has not increased. Stocks of munitions and spare parts, training and recruitment, and consequently combat readiness of units and equipment, have all suffered as a result of the budget crunch and the continuous rapid pace of international deployments, including in the Baltic States, Mali, Jordan, Afghanistan and Iraq. Echoing public sentiment, the AIV considers these shortfalls a serious problem: the Netherlands must consider the possibility that, in response to the

---

15 Netherlands Ministry of Foreign Affairs, 'Turbulent Times in Unstable Surroundings', pp. 11–12.

16 AIV, 'De Toekomst Van De Navo En De Veiligheid Van Europa' ['The Future of NATO and the Security of Europe'], October 2017, pp. 25–31; Kristin ven Bruusgaard, 'Russian Strategic Deterrence', *Survival* (Vol. 58, No. 4, 2016), pp. 7–26; Stephan Frühling and Guillaume Lasconjarias, 'NATO, A2/AD and the Kaliningrad Challenge', *Survival* (Vol. 58, No. 2, 2016), pp. 95–116; Elbridge Colby and Jonathan Solomon, 'Facing Russia: Conventional Defence and Deterrence in Europe', *Survival* (Vol. 57, No. 6, 2015), pp. 21–50.

military challenge posed by Russia, NATO will ask more from the Dutch armed forces than they have provided in past and current operations. Neither can future deployment in the Middle East and North Africa be ruled out.[17]

In 2017, the Cabinet confirmed rumours that it intended to increase defence spending by €1.5 billion annually and aim, in due course, to reach the European average as a percentage of GDP. Analysts publicly advised the Ministry of Defence to solve the readiness problem and prioritise collective defence and capabilities relevant to the A2AD problem.[18] Service chiefs agreed. Internal debates ensued within the Ministry of Defence leadership about spending priorities. The army, understandably, favoured regaining armoured capabilities. The air force stressed the importance of the intelligence, surveillance, and reconnaissance (ISR) and stealth capabilities of the F-35. Pointing out that its F-16s had seen continuous deployment for almost 25 years, it warned that 37 F-35s would only be capable of sustaining a contribution of four aircraft to prolonged deployments. In addition, ongoing operations had demonstrated the need to expand the transport-helicopter fleet. The navy emphasised that it had to replace its ageing submarine and frigate fleet. Early in 2018, the newly appointed minister of defence emphasised that cyber and intelligence capabilities also required expansion.

The Integrated Foreign and Security Strategy: Business as Usual?

Russia's actions had, however, not altered the wide geographical scope of the foreign, security and defence policy of the Netherlands. In March 2018, the Ministry of Foreign Affairs (MFA) published its long-awaited Integrated International and Security Strategy (IISS), tellingly entitled 'Worldwide for a Secure Netherlands'.[19] The IISS rests on three pillars: prevent; defend; and strengthen. It contains entirely sensible observations, reflecting insights and trends from reports cited in this chapter, and announces a substantial range of sound measures to promote security. It

---

17 AIV, 'Instability Around Europe', p. 33.

18 See van Veldhuizen et al., *Geopolitiek en Defensie*; Scientific Advisory Counsel, *Veiligheid in een wereld van verbindingen: een strategische visie op het defensiebeleid* [*Security in a Connected World: A Strategic Perspective on Defence Policy*], Report No. 98 (The Hague: WRR, 2017).

19 Government of the Netherlands, Geïntegreerde Buitenland- en Veiligheidsstrategie 2018–2022 [Integrated International and Security Strategy 2018–2022], 'Wereldwijd voor een veilig Nederland' ['Worldwide for a Secure Netherlands'], March 2018, <https://www.rijksoverheid.nl/actueel/nieuws/2018/03/20/wereldwijd-voor-een-veilig-nederland—geintegreerde-buitenland–en-veiligheidsstrategie-2018-2022>, accessed 18 July 2018.

recognises four trends, six urgent threats, and thirteen goals and policy measures.

The first trend is that the West is entering a 'multi-order world' which will make international cooperation and the effective functioning of established international organisations more difficult. The second trend is increasing instability and threats in Europe and the Caribbean. The third trend is the accelerating pace of technological development and the potential that modern technology allows states and non-state actors to engage in hybrid conflict with the West. The fourth trend is increasing societal tensions which threaten the democratic foundations of European states.

These trends form tangible threats which, in order of priority, the IISS lists as:

- Terrorist attacks.
- Cyber threats.
- Unwanted foreign influence.
- Military threats against the Netherlands and NATO territory (including the possible use of nuclear weapons).
- Threats to vital economic processes.
- Chemical, biological, radiological and nuclear capabilities.

While including a broad, balanced perspective on security, and acknowledging the geographical reality that the European continent is increasingly threatened, the IISS does not communicate the same sense of urgency and geopolitical focus as the 2015 letter, and instead adopts a more general perspective when it addresses the 'how' of the strategy. The first plank in the strategy – prevent – is about goals preventing conflict around Europe and the Caribbean, removing the sources of terrorism (focusing in particular on the Middle East and Africa), promoting disarmament and non-proliferation of weapons of mass destruction, and setting international norms for cyber activities. In its second and third planks – defend and strengthen – the strategy also maintains a broad geographic perspective. It stresses goals such as countering cross-border criminal activities, bolstering societal resilience, protecting economic security, combating terrorism, and investing in cyber intelligence and offensive cyber capabilities. The IISS expects that UN peacekeeping operations, counter-piracy operations, crisis management operations, and combat missions such as the ongoing campaign against Daesh, will all continue and probably expand, be more frequent, and require patience and endurance. According to the strategy, these operations contribute to sustaining the international order and stability in the regions surrounding Europe, and thus foster security in Europe.

A focus on Europe itself comes to the fore when the strategy discusses NATO. But here in particular the strategy embodies the diversity of interests and priorities within the MFA, the difference in perspective between the Ministry of Defence and the MFA, and the diverse opinions of the parties within the coalition Cabinet. Whereas the Ministry of Defence favours more emphasis on Russia, the military dimension of security, and collective defence, the MFA prefers retaining some of the dominant features of previous policies and practices which emphasise, for instance, development and human rights. Subsequently, the IISS notes (somewhat in tension with international analysis, the 2017 AIV report, the 2017 Telders Stichting study and the 2017 report of the Scientific Council for Government Policy) that collective defence should regain its priority alongside crisis management and capacity-building in developing countries – both of which, according to the strategy, retain high priority as they must be considered a form of 'forward defence'. Reaching this goal requires renewed attention to deterrence (conventional, nuclear and cyber), modernising defensive capabilities, and improving readiness and sustainment capabilities.

The 2018 Defence White Paper: Change or Continuity?

Almost at the same time as the publication of the IISS, the Cabinet presented its plans for the armed forces. In some respects, the Ministry of Defence White Paper, 'Investing in our People, Capabilities and Visibility',[20] incorporates calls made in earlier advisory reports to increase defence spending and echoes the warning about Russia. It predicts that the situation on NATO's eastern flank will call for rapidly deployable, robust military units of substantial size, and that the defence budget will, by 2021, structurally have increased by a substantial total of €1.5 billion. It also shares the security outlook of the IISS and anticipates that NATO will call upon the Netherlands' armed forces to meet NATO capability goals. More than the IISS does, it admits that collective defence of NATO is increasingly important. The paper advocates that the Netherlands sustain its commitment to the mission against Daesh and to NATO's reassurance initiatives in Eastern Europe. In addition, it aims to foster 'flow security': safeguarding the integrity of vital infrastructure and access to and use of

[20] Ministry of Defence, 'Investing in our People, Capabilities and Visibility', 2018, <https://www.rijksoverheid.nl/documenten/rapporten/2018/03/26/defensienota-2018-investeren-in-onze-mensen-slagkracht-en-zichtbaarheid>, accessed 18 July 2018.

economic lines of communication. The paper states that stabilisation missions in the Middle East, North Africa and parts of sub-Saharan and West Africa will continue to demand attention. Combined with the continued efforts to foster international stability (with which it echoes the IISS) and internal security activities, this will likely result in a more intense pace of deployments.[21]

On the other hand, the paper acknowledges that the new defence budget will amount to just 1.28 per cent of GDP in 2021. According to the minister of defence, the glass is half full;[22] therefore, she admitted, this white paper must be regarded as merely a first step towards achieving the 2 per cent target (which would amount to an increase of about €6 billion annually) by 2024. The current increase is insufficient to allow the Ministry of Defence to break significantly with previous policy. Force modernisation is required not only in light of Russian modernisation, but also in light of new technologies including big data, artificial intelligence, robotics and biotechnology. Further, the Ministry of Defence is forced to limit its ambitions to restore the combat readiness of units, their personal equipment, combat-support capabilities, and weapon systems, all of which have suffered from years of intense deployments and increased wear and tear. In terms of substantial capability development, the budget only allows for the long-planned replacement of ageing frigates, submarines and mine-countermeasure vessels. Investments in cyber and intelligence capabilities will increase gradually. The army will reconstitute its artillery capabilities and, through cooperation with the German army, maintain its capability to conduct combined-arms operations. Three Chinook helicopters will be added to the fleet and the air force will, after years of postponement, finally acquire and introduce the Reaper ISR drone. Recruitment and retention of personnel, as the title of the white paper suggests, is also an area of focus, as the army in particular is experiencing difficulties in filling its units. Overall, the Ministry of Defence is unable to staff about 8,000 positions, which equates to approximately 15 per cent of its entire personnel capacity.[23]

Despite the wide geographical perspective of its missions, the actual capability of the Netherlands' armed forces thus remains very limited. As the white paper illustrates in summary: the army aims to sustain a brigade-level task force for a short-duration mission, or a battalion-sized contribution for missions of longer duration; the navy seeks to be able to

---

21 *Ibid.*, pp. 8–11.

22 As quoted by Joris Jansen Lok, 'De Toekomst van Defensie' ['The Future of Defence'], *Onze Luchtmacht* [*Our Air Force*] (No. 1, 2018), p. 2.

23 Marc de Natris, 'Mooie woorden omzetten in zichtbare daden' ['Turn Nice Words into Visible Action'], *ProDef Bulletin* (No. 3, May 2018), p. 1.

contribute five ships to short-duration collective defence operations or two surface vessels to a mission of longer duration; the air force, once the F-35 reaches operational status, is expected to contribute four fighters to long-duration missions.[24] The white paper therefore hardly reflects the requirements of 'the new normal'. More is needed, commentators argue.[25] One influential analyst cynically commented that both the white paper and the state of the armed forces were beyond hope.[26]

Conclusion

The shock of 2014 was, tragically, strategically informative in convincing Europe that old ghosts have returned, and hard power is still essential on the continent. NATO's array of initiatives since 2014 amounts to rediscovering the lost art of conventional and nuclear deterrence, territorial defence and conventional warfare. That is the 'no-surprise' baseline security environment. While the future is uncertain, defence planners and politicians must now take the certainty seriously that Europe's militaries should be prepared for both wars of choice and wars of necessity. The white papers recently published in the Netherlands recognise the European security predicament but fail to prioritise resources accordingly.

Certainly, the security of Northern Europe matters. On 7 June 2018, the minister of defence welcomed her colleagues from the Northern Group, highlighting the importance of enhanced cooperation in that region vis-à-vis an assertive Russia.[27] Existing commitments to the defence of Northern Europe will also continue. A troop contingent of 270 will continue to be part of NATO's multinational battlegroup stationed in Rukla, Lithuania. Dutch brigades will continue to prepare for and participate in Article 5 operational exercises, such as the international

---

[24] Ministry of Defence, 'Investing in our People, Capabilities and Visibility', pp. 17–18. See, for a similar pessimistic assessment, Rob de Wijk, 'De veiligheidsanalyse is er, nu nog de middelen' ['The Security Analysis is There, Now for the Capabilities'], *Trouw*, 30 March 2018.

[25] See, for instance, Eric Vrijsen, 'Krijgsmacht is zo chronisch verwaarloosd dat 1,5 miljard zo op is' ['The Armed Forces Have Been so Chronically Neglected, 1.5 Billion Will be Spent in No Time'], *Elsevier*, 28 March 2018; Ton Welter, 'Tweede Kamer moet verhoogd budget voor defensie veiligstellen' ['Parliament Must Ensure Longterm Increase of Defence Budget'], *Elsevier*, 22 May 2018; Jan Jonker and Olaf van Jooren, 'Er moet nog (veel) meer geld bij' ['(Much) More Money is Required'], *De Telegraaf*, 27 March 2018, p. T8.

[26] Jansen Lok, 'De Toekomst van Defensie'.

[27] Ministry of Defence, 'Noordelijke partners bespreken dreiging Rusland' ['Northern Partners Discuss Russia Threat'], Communiqué, 7 June 2018, <https://www.defensie.nl/actueel/nieuws>, accessed 23 July 2018.

brigade-level exercise *Bison Drawsko* in Poland in 2017. Dutch submarines (old and new), frigates and minesweepers will patrol the North Atlantic and the North Sea as part of NATO's Standing Maritime units. The army is also committed to NATO's VJTF and Initial Follow-On Forces Group with a mechanised-infantry battalion, an anti-tank company, a field-artillery battery, a reconnaissance platoon, and staff to man the brigade headquarters. The German/Netherlands Corps stands ready to provide a Joint Task Force Headquarters. The air force has committed four F-16s to air policing in the Baltics, also as part of the VJTF, with an additional four fighter aircraft ready to support long-duration operations.

On the other hand, the new integrated security policy, important as the first of its kind, while informed by threats and risks to Europe, maintains an almost-global perspective and a broad approach to achieving security. The military dimension of European security is not a central feature. Compared to previous papers produced by the MFA since 2014, it also suggests the government is less alarmed than it was in 2015. Deliberately linked to that strategy, the 2018 defence white paper, in turn, while fully cognisant of the strategic challenges ahead, admits that, financially, the Ministry of Defence will for a while fall short of properly responding to the new international security environment. Plans do little or nothing to prepare the Netherlands' armed forces to help remedy the European capability gap, or contribute to fostering Europe's strategic autonomy. The impact of 25 years of budget cuts, combined with continuous deployments, will take longer to reverse.[28]

Therefore, the AIV assessment of 2015 that 'Dutch contributions to missions cannot disguise the fact that for a considerable time the Dutch armed forces have not met the requirement of full-spectrum deployability, while sizeable units are barely capable of sustained operations',[29] will hold true for the next four years. In the most recent defence white paper, the Ministry of Defence states the aspiration that the situation will have improved by 2024. By then a full decade will have passed since the watershed year of 2014.

---

[28] Ruud Vermeulen, 'De Defensienota in Perspectief' ['The Defence Memorandum in Perspective'], *ProDef Bulletin* (No. 3, May 2018), pp. 2–3.

[29] AIV, 'Instability Around Europe'.

VII. POLAND: NATO'S FRONT LINE STATE

MARCIN ZABOROWSKI

As Poland approaches its twentieth anniversary as a member of NATO, the sense of insecurity at the Alliance's eastern flank is growing. When Poland joined the Alliance in 1999, the dominant perception was that NATO would provide Poland with full security guarantees. Over subsequent years, as NATO focused on out-of-area missions, Poland was determined to demonstrate to its Western allies that it could act as a security provider. However, since Russia's invasion of Ukraine, Poland has led the argument in favour of boosting the Alliance's presence on its eastern flank. Decisions taken at the NATO Warsaw Summit in 2016 went some way to meeting these expectations, but fell short of providing the eastern flank with adequate deterrence.

The war in Ukraine has put Poland back into its historical geopolitical dilemma as a state in an unstable security environment and lacking meaningful natural borders to hamper a large-scale conventional invasion. Poland's sovereign statehood, built around the principle of rejoining the West, may be directly threatened as the result of Russia's actions in Ukraine, the expansion of Russian nuclear capabilities in the Kaliningrad exclave that directly borders Poland, and the increase in military incidents in the air and waters of Northern Europe.

In essence, this means that Poland has again become a front line state, which certainly narrows its diplomatic options, although its relative importance for the West could grow. As Russia's military build-up in Kaliningrad and its aggressive exercises (which include simulated nuclear attacks on Warsaw) intensify, Poland will naturally prioritise its own security and the security of its nearest allies, particularly in the Baltic. While over the last ten to fifteen years, Warsaw was expected to show its commitment to making a mark beyond its immediate neighbourhood –

and did so militarily in Iraq and Afghanistan and politically by sharing its experience of democratisation – it is not surprising that such activities will now decline. Russia's aggressive posture is therefore successfully preventing Poland from becoming an outward-looking actor, but it also makes Poland more central to the Western alliance. Following the developments of the last years, Poland is also becoming increasingly tied to the Baltic–Nordic region. Warsaw's future defence policy is now intimately connected to that of the entire region and this trend is likely to grow.

Returning to Front Line Status

Russia has boosted its military capabilities in the Kaliningrad region and it has caused a number of military incidents in the Baltic region. Russia has been carrying out large propaganda efforts in the Baltic States and the Visegrad countries and its espionage activities have intensified. Until recently, the US and its NATO allies assumed that although Russia could be a nuisance, it was not an active military threat. At least until the outbreak of the war in Ukraine, many believed, with good reason, that the challenges to Russian security now came from China and Central Asia and that Russia's rapprochement with the West would only be a matter of time.[1]

These assumptions often meant that the role defined for NATO during the Cold War as the provider of security in Europe was no longer seen as central, if at all relevant. Leaders, therefore, argued that the Alliance had to refocus to become a stability provider (in the Balkans) or peace enforcer (in Afghanistan). The defence of Europe against the prospect of Russian aggression was, and in many circles is still, seen as an obsolete task for NATO.[2] Russia's war with Georgia in 2008 failed to change this perspective, although some in the strategic community began to sound the alarm. Only since Russia's 2014 annexation of Crimea have Western perceptions of Russia started to alter. Following the annexation of Crimea, Russia continues to execute and sponsor aggressive actions in the east of Ukraine in close proximity to NATO member states.[3]

[1] One of the prime examples of this thinking was put forward by Barack Obama's deputy national security advisor, Charles Kupchan, in Charles Kupchan, 'NATO's Final Frontier: Why Russia Should Join the Atlantic Alliance', *Foreign Affairs* (May/June 2010).

[2] *Ibid.*; for the evolution of NATO's perception of the relationship with Russia, see also Karl-Heinz Kamp, 'Why NATO Needs a New Strategic Concept', NATO Defense College Foundation, November 2016.

[3] See Michael Koffman et al., *Lessons from Russia's Operations in Crimea and Eastern Ukraine* (Santa Monica, CA: RAND Corporation, 2017).

Poland and its NATO allies would be unwise to close their eyes to the fact that Putin's Russia is a belligerent power that at the moment represents the greatest threat to the security of Europe. Recognising this should have immediate implications for the way NATO positions its forces and builds credible deterrence. Poland should make a greater effort to acquire front line state capabilities and position its forces along its eastern border. NATO and the US should also invest in the security of Poland, which, as a front line state, is assuming a major role for the entire Alliance and the role of the US in Europe, as indeed stipulated by the contingency plans that foresee a major role for Polish armed forces in case of a direct threat to the Baltic region.

Following the Alliance's decisions taken at the Warsaw Summit, Poland and the Baltic States have hosted 4,500 NATO troops in the framework of the Enhanced Forward Presence (EFP). Additionally, the US 2nd Armoured Brigade Combat Team and 1st Infantry Division headquarters have been stationed in Poland.

Implications for the US and NATO

The US established and maintained its post-war position in no small part through the system of privileged relations with front line states: Japan and South Korea in Asia; the UK, Germany, Italy and Turkey in Europe; and the Gulf States in the Middle East. In each, the US has established military bases and bilateral status of forces agreements. Since the end of the Cold War, US perceptions of Europe as a potential battleground declined sharply and with them the presence of US forces, which have been reduced from their Cold War strength of 340,000 to the approximately 30,000 that remained in 2015.[4]

The Ukraine crisis has altered this strategic picture, with rather small but nonetheless meaningful material consequences. As noted, NATO has established some rotational presence in front line Poland and the Baltic States, but it is unclear whether this constitutes meaningful deterrence. When the modalities of the presence were discussed and agreed upon, its initial purpose was to reassure the eastern flank Allies, Poland included. At the same time, the US presence in Western Europe is a fraction of what it had been at the height of the Cold War.

[4] According to the official document of US Command in Europe, at the height of the Cold War, more than 400,000 US forces were stationed across 100 communities on the European continent. Today, US forces on the continent have been reduced by more than 85 per cent, See US European Command, 'US Military Presence in Europe (1945-2016)', May 2016, <www.eucom.mil/doc/35220/u-s-forces-in-europe>, accessed 23 July 2018.

This suggests that, at the time of writing, the US administration has not fully come to perceive the Ukraine crisis and Russia's growing assertiveness as a challenge to its role in Europe and in the world. Alternatively, it might indicate that even if the administration were aware of the problem presented by Russia, the US is unable to act due to resource constraints and a growing number of challenges in other parts of the world, in particular, northeast Asia and the Middle East. However, further delay in recognising and acting on the new political reality in Central and Eastern Europe may prove costly for the US, particularly if Russia decides to push its confrontational activities into NATO territory and the Baltic States. It is therefore only a matter of time before the US needs to either recognise Poland and the Baltic States as front line areas or abdicate from the role it has filled in Europe since the end of the Second World War.

In practice, the former option would need an investment in terms of US forces in Central and Eastern Europe. As resource constraints are likely to continue for some time, the US may decide to relocate some of the forces it maintains in Western Europe to the front line areas. In any case, there is no doubt that the Poles and the Baltic States would welcome greater US military presence. In fact, the Poles have even offered to pay $2 billion for setting up a permanent US base on Polish territory. As of now, the prospects for accepting the Polish offer are however rather dim as there is no consensus within NATO to press ahead with a permanent presence that is seen as violating the NATO–Russia Founding Act.

Redefining Poland's Role as an Ally

As Poland joined NATO in 1999, the Alliance was embarking on its first-ever intervention in Kosovo. Since then, NATO has concentrated on redefining its role beyond collective defence. In reality, that meant that the role of defending NATO territory started to be viewed as somehow archaic, and the Alliance was instead expected to focus its efforts on out-of-area operations aimed first and foremost at peacekeeping and peace enforcement. In NATO headquarters 'deterrence' and 'territorial defence' became controversial terms associated with old-fashioned Cold War thinking.

This evolution had major implications for planning processes. The leading European NATO powers – the UK and France, followed closely by Germany – issued white papers that advocated abandoning the focus on territorial defence and instead investing in expeditionary capabilities. States such as Poland that were reluctant to embrace this trend were criticised for a preoccupation with territorial defence and insufficient investment in expeditionary capabilities.[5] Meanwhile, the UK, France and Germany, and then other NATO allies were drastically reducing their armoured capabilities. Almost all European allies, Poland included, abandoned conscription, switching to much smaller all-volunteer forces. At the same time, the investment in developing expeditionary capabilities came slowly. A number of European NATO allies cancelled their orders for next-generation strategic airlift, while France and the UK failed to reach agreement on developing a joint transport aircraft. While some investment in expeditionary capabilities did materialise, overall defence spending was declining until the Ukraine crisis.[6]

Like other NATO members, Poland was expected to follow this course. Indeed, Warsaw proved one of the most active participants in out-of-area missions, becoming one of the major contributors to the operations in Iraq (providing more than 3,000 troops) and Afghanistan (2,500 troops). Participation in these and other operations motivated Poland's armed forces to modernise and has also had the benefit of identifying some obvious technical inadequacies. It was also an important show of solidarity with the US. But the investment made in those missions has meant that Poland spent a considerable share of its resources on operations not directly linked to Poland's own security needs. This led to a certain backlash in public opinion, which turned critical towards Poland's participation in overseas missions. That sentiment filtered into leadership views and influenced Poland's decision not to participate in NATO's operation in Libya, as well as prompting vocal criticism in Warsaw about the prospect of an Allied operation in Syria (which never materialised).

As Russia entered into a war in Georgia in 2008, annexed Crimea in 2014 and then moved into eastern Ukraine, it became clear that redirecting the Alliance's mission away from the core task of defending its territory was premature. Some NATO members have already reacted to the new reality. Lithuania reintroduced conscription; all the Baltic States have raised their levels of defence spending; many other nations have halted defence cuts. Meanwhile, Poland announced that it was embarking on an ambitious plan of investing in its defensive capabilities that includes

---

5 French Ministry of Defence, 'French White Paper: Defence and National Security', July 2013, <https://www.defense.gouv.fr/content/download/215253/2394121/White%2520paper%2520on%2520defense%2520%25202013.pdf+&cd=2&hl=pl&ct=clnk&gl=pl&client=safari>, accessed 23 July 2018; HM Government, *National Security Strategy and Strategic Defence and Security Review 2015: A Secure and Prosperous United Kingdom*, Cm9161 (London: The Stationery Office, 2015).

6 For figures on Poland's defence spending, see Marcin Zaborowski, 'Poland and European Defense Integration', ECFR Policy Brief, January 2018, <http://www.ecfr.eu/publications/summary/poland_and_european_defence_integration>, accessed 23 July 2018.

the development of an air and missile defence system, as well as the acquisition of attack and transport helicopters and submarines.[7] The programme was in fact discussed before the Ukraine crisis erupted, but no doubt the developments beyond Poland's eastern border gave an additional urgency to these investments.

As Poland invests in these new capabilities, it is important that it do so to the benefit of the entire Alliance. As a front line state, Poland has additional responsibilities, but NATO should also recognise that Poland and the Baltic States are potential battlegrounds and that as such their primary value lies in effectively protecting the eastern frontier of the Alliance. To fulfil this purpose, the front line states need capable and well-equipped forces.

Poland's armed forces have made great progress since the outset of the transition, evolving from a large conscription-based force of more than 350,000 troops to an all-volunteer force of just over 100,000. The ongoing modernisation programme, along with the consistent growth in defence spending, has had a positive impact on the quality of Poland's armed forces. However, some areas suffer from considerable shortfalls resulting from the legacy of the communist period. For example, a majority of the forces remain stationed along Poland's western border while the eastern border is insufficiently protected. The reduction in the number of active-duty personnel has been too deep and the current force is insufficient to effectively protect NATO's eastern frontier. Geography – wide-open plains stretching between Poland and its eastern neighbours – and geopolitics suggest that Poland should organise its armed forces to focus on a land-warfare scenario. Poland's NATO allies, in particular, the US, would do well to recognise this.

The EU Dimension

Poland's security policy rests first and foremost on NATO and Warsaw's close relationship with the US. However, as the EU develops its defence arm, Poland will increasingly face the need to respond to European initiatives. This has both political and economic implications. To date, Poland has alternated between strongly pro-EU positions and the current, rather sceptical position.

Under the government of 2008–15, Poland acquired a reputation as a Europhile state quickly catching up with the rest of the EU. During this period, Warsaw's enthusiasm for the EU extended to defence, prompting it to join Germany and France as one of the main sponsors of defence integration. The Polish government advocated the development of

[7] *Ibid.*

Permanent Structured Cooperation (PESCO) and a planning headquarters for EU operations. Warsaw also signed up to the Eurocorps and participated in numerous EU operations from Africa to Georgia. However, since the election of a Eurosceptic government, Warsaw's attitude towards European defence initiatives has been at best lukewarm and on occasion openly hostile.

Under its current administration, Poland has been reluctant to engage in EU defence cooperation, including defence industrial. Political and personal considerations largely drive the scepticism of Polish leaders regarding EU attempts to develop genuine defence cooperation. After months of criticising the launch of PESCO and failing to reach a decision, Warsaw became one of the last member states to signal its intention to join the initiative. It did so with an evident lack of enthusiasm, eventually deciding to participate only to slow, and possibly even wreck, the undertaking. Thus, Warsaw signed up to just two of PESCO's seventeen projects: those for developing software-defined radio and for simplifying and standardising cross-border military-transport procedures. Neither of these projects is central to the initiative, but each potentially enables Warsaw to block progress. This stands in stark contrast to the behaviour of the previous Polish government that was part of the vanguard of European defence.

Embarking on European defence-industrial cooperation certainly carries risks. Poland's state-owned defence group PGZ is in no position to compete effectively against Western European defence giants. In the absence of effective safeguards, a Polish company that enters into a joint venture with a larger European firm could be subjected to a de facto takeover that reduces its role to that of a subcontractor. However, these risks are equally, if not more, acute in comparable arrangements with American defence companies, which traditionally keep co-production to a minimum and refuse to transfer the most advanced technologies to their partners. Poland's experience with procuring F-16s in 2002 shows that offset provisions can be left largely unfulfilled once the order is placed, and this substantial procurement has yielded no measurable benefits for Polish defence companies. If the trends evident in late 2017 continue, it is likely that the procurement of Patriot missile systems from Raytheon, already confirmed by the current government, will repeat this experience. Again, Poland's dilemma has precedent. During the Cold War, Western European countries seeking to rearm and rebuild industrial capacity implemented 'buy American' defence-procurement policies; only those that did so in an intelligent fashion developed a strong industrial base.[8]

---

[8] Jean Belin et al., 'Defense Industrial Links between EU and the US', ARES Papers, September 2017, <http://www.iris-france.org/wp-content/uploads/2017/09/Ares-20-Report-EU-DTIB-Sept-2017.pdf>, accessed 23 July 2018.

Governments that are serious about national security cannot afford to let their defence industry drift, nor rely only on orders from external contractors. Poland is still catching up with the rest of the EU and its technological base remains weak. The current situation offers a chance for the defence industry to become an engine of broader modernisation. While the risks of cooperation are real, the dangers stemming from a failure to cooperate are greater. Largely unreformed, underfinanced and lacking in technological capability, PGZ cannot meet the imperative to modernise as long as its only significant contractor, the Ministry of Defence, is also its owner.[9] Therefore, the group would benefit from smart cooperation with foreign partners that would allow it to gain access to advanced technologies and export markets without losing its distinctive character. The government's support for the defence industry is both well placed and no different from that applied in other EU states. However, a mismanaged and unreformed industry will not improve on its own, and the relative security of government orders provides little incentive to modernise. While protecting its independence, the industry should enter into partnerships with foreign firms that provide not just ready-made products or assembly lines, but also the kind of investment that can help modernise domestic production.

The Baltic–Nordic Dimension

Poland is not the only front line state in both the EU and NATO context: the entire Baltic–Nordic region is exposed to the Russian threat. Following the Russian annexation of Crimea, the region has experienced numerous military incidents involving Russian aircraft or submarines. Many consider scenarios of the partial or complete takeover of the Baltic States by the Russian military or Russian-sponsored separatists as the next steps in Putin's anti-West strategy. Indeed, since 2014 separatist activity in the Baltic States has intensified as the result of Russian propaganda efforts. The Russian FSB kidnapped an Estonian intelligence officer, and numerous border violation incidents have occurred. There can be no doubt that the Baltic–Nordic region is particularly vulnerable and exposed.

Poland holds a unique position in this regional context. Geographically, it is a part of the Baltic region, but politically it has a different status and different resources from the Baltic States. Until relatively recently, NATO performed no contingency planning for potential Russian operations in the Baltic, but current plans envisage a major role for the Polish military in coming to the defence of the Baltic

9 Zaborowski, 'Poland and European Defense Integration'.

States in case of Russian aggression. Poland also regularly takes part in Baltic Air Policing missions and has security arrangements with all the Baltic States. Like the Nordic countries, Poland serves as a security provider in the region. Poland works particularly closely in the defence sector with Lithuania, with which it even formed a trilateral brigade that also includes Ukrainian forces.

As Edward Lucas argues, the Baltic–Nordic region could, in fact, defend itself effectively against Russian aggression.[10] The region's combined GDP is higher than Russia's and its combined military resources are significant. However, the region's military potential suffers from divisions, with some states not being NATO members (Sweden and Finland), some not belonging to the EU (Norway and Iceland), and all having a different degree of exposure to the Russian threat. The existing security and defence cooperation organisation of the Nordics, NORDEFCO, definitely represents a step in the right direction, but it does not include the Baltic States or Poland.

As Poland's role in the NATO context is increasingly tied to the Baltic States, Warsaw is likely to look for ways to strengthen regional cooperation through arrangements either with individual states or with a group of states. In terms of military strategy, Poland is in the process or reorganising its forces with a view to engaging in the Baltic region and defending its eastern border.

Future Directions

After securing its membership in NATO and the EU, Poland had its 'end of history' moment. Many believed that Poland was now safe and that thanks to the EU it would steadily become more prosperous. With democracy and a market economy seemingly secured at home, Poland began to look outward. That perception resulted in the transformation of the armed forces, the end of conscription and participation in a number of overseas missions. Prior to the Ukraine crisis and following US President Barack Obama's 'reset' policy, Poland was also taking steps toward rapprochement with Russia. The Polish government at the time believed that the historically acrimonious relations between the two countries could undergo a process similar to the one that Poland experienced with Germany after the end of the Cold War.

The prospect of finding a *modus vivendi* with Russia allowed Poland to seek a role outside its immediate area of interest, which resulted in Poland's participation in EU stabilisation missions in sub-Saharan Africa, the Democratic Republic of the Congo and Chad, and its activism in offering its know-how in political transitions in Tunisia and Myanmar.

[10] Edward Lucas, 'The Coming Storm: Baltic Sea Security Report', CEPA Paper, Centre for European Policy Analysis, June 2015, <https://www.cepa.org/the-coming-storm>, accessed 23 July 2018.

Warsaw's foreign policy under the leadership of former Prime Minister Donald Tusk and Foreign Minister Radoslaw Sikorski was evidently becoming more global. However, Russia's annexation of Crimea and its war in Eastern Ukraine have reminded Poland that its security environment remains predatory and that Warsaw cannot afford the luxury of spreading its resources too thin. Therefore, although Poland would have wished to depart from the logic of being a front line state, it cannot do so. Instead, it will have to concentrate on securing its own terrain and on the Baltic region, becoming perhaps even more tied to this region than it has been so far.

Recognising Poland as a front line state, NATO should invest significant military resources and personnel in Poland. Working together with the Polish government, the US and other NATO allies should develop effective deterrence in and around the Baltic area. It is often argued now that the area is already covered by 'extended deterrence' – meaning conventional and nuclear capabilities that exist in Western Europe and could strike an aggressor in the aftermath of an attack. However, as the success of Russia's hybrid-warfare methods in Ukraine have demonstrated, the only truly credible deterrent discourages the aggressor from taking action in the first place. The substantial presence of US and Allied troops in Poland and the Baltic States should fulfil that purpose. NATO's EFP and US deployments in Poland are definitely steps in the right direction in this context.

Conclusion

Poland's real contribution to Western security lies in its role of defending NATO's eastern frontier and the Baltic region. In the past, NATO has pushed Poland to participate in overseas missions and acquire capabilities allowing it to execute operations in remote parts of the world. At present, encouraging Poland to concentrate on itself and the Baltic Sea would make more strategic sense. Poland's eastern border lacks natural barriers and is therefore difficult to defend, requiring the presence of large land forces and mechanised divisions. As Poland transforms its armed forces, NATO should help it to concentrate on acquiring the capabilities necessary in such scenarios.

As a front line state, Poland should gain preferential status for the American and European defence industry. Poland has become one of the prime buyers of US defence equipment in Europe, but to date, US defence companies have made only meagre investments in Poland. A major investment contributing to Poland's technological development would certainly give greater substance to the relationship and could boost the front line state's own capabilities.

VIII. DEFENCE AND SECURITY IN NORTHERN EUROPE: A WASHINGTON VIEW

ALEXANDER VERSHBOW AND
MAGNUS NORDENMAN

The US defence and security relationship with the states of Northern Europe has evolved significantly over time, transitioning from the Cold War view of those countries as the northern flank of NATO into a recognition of these states as a group of small but capable partners in post-Cold War expeditionary operations. Today, however, US engagement in Northern Europe and relationships with its allies and partners are once again changing, as the region has become a key zone of friction with Russia under President Vladimir Putin, intent on altering the European security order in Moscow's favour. The US has accomplished much since 2014 in terms of strengthening presence and engagement in the region as well as deepening defence cooperation with Norway, Denmark, Sweden, Finland, Estonia, Latvia, Lithuania, Poland, Germany, and others in Northern Europe. However, the US and Northern Europe must further enhance their defence and security arrangements both bilaterally and multilaterally, including within the context of NATO.

Northern Europe from a Washington Perspective

From a US defence and security perspective, Northern Europe consists of two distinct but interlinked regions: the Baltic Sea region, which today includes both NATO members and close partners; and the Atlantic-facing part of Northern Europe, which also encompasses the European Arctic, or High North. Given their geography, these two regions have different security concerns. The maritime domain naturally dominates the defence calculations of the Atlantic-facing part of Northern Europe, while the Baltic Sea region, in spite of its label, focuses primarily on threats in the air and ground domains. Moreover, in a regional context, the priorities of Sweden, Finland, the Baltic States, Poland, and Germany focus primarily on the Baltic Sea, while Norway, the UK and the Netherlands naturally take a greater interest in the North Atlantic region. Denmark shares the priorities of both regions due to Danish sovereignty over Greenland.

The Baltic region now includes three Baltic States and Poland as NATO front line allies in the new contest between Russia and the West. Given their small size, limited resource base and location, and the advantage Russia enjoys in terms of time and distance required for access, the Baltic States also present an especially difficult, but not impossible, defence problem for the US and NATO.[1]

The Atlantic-facing portion of Northern Europe, including the High North, constitutes NATO's northern flank, and the ability to defend and control it during a crisis will be vital to ensuring the rapid reinforcement of NATO from the US across the Atlantic. Few expect a crisis involving NATO and Russia to begin in the High North, but the region could quickly become a theatre of operations in a conflict escalating from, for example, the Baltic Sea region, as Russia would seek to use its powerful Northern Fleet to deny the maritime domain north of the Greenland–Iceland–UK (GIUK) gap to NATO and US forces.[2]

To the Ends of the Earth and Back

To understand the challenges and opportunities facing the US and its friends, allies and partners in Northern Europe as they seek to build effective deterrence in the new security environment, it is important to understand the evolution of the US relationship with the states in the region over the last 30 years. In the post-Cold War period, Europe's northeast – Estonia, Latvia, Lithuania and Poland – transformed from a collection of Soviet satellite states into full NATO and EU members. This was no small feat considering the fragile economic and political position in which these states found themselves in the early 1990s, and that Russian forces retained a presence in the Baltic States for several years after independence. The successful transition was significantly aided by the US working closely with its allies and partners in Northern Europe while engaging in creative diplomacy with Moscow. Furthermore, the US, in

1 See, for example, David Shlapak and Michael Johnson, *Reinforcing Deterrence on NATO's Eastern Flank* (Santa Monica, CA: RAND Corporation, 2016).

2 Magnus Nordenman, 'Back to the Gap: The Re-Emerging Maritime Contest in the North Atlantic', *RUSI Journal* (Vol. 162, No. 1, February/March 2017), pp. 24–30.

cooperation with its Nordic partners and allies, made significant contributions to the creation and early development of the Baltic armed forces, including training, education and the transfer of basic equipment.[3]

Meanwhile, Denmark and Norway became partners of choice for Washington in several out-of-area operations that represented the raison d'être of NATO that had emerged in the 1990s, especially in the wake of the 9/11 attacks on the US. This shift towards expeditionary operations was especially pronounced in Copenhagen, with Danish forces taking on difficult combat missions in Afghanistan and Iraq. Washington praised both Norway and Denmark for the strong military contributions of these relatively small states, especially during Operation *Active Endeavour* in the skies over Libya in 2011.

Sweden and Finland, states that for political and geographic reasons remained outside NATO during the Cold War, expanded and deepened their own defence and security relationships with both the US and NATO by contributing forces to NATO-led peacekeeping operations in the Balkans and to the International Security Assistance Force mission in Afghanistan. Finland also made considerable investments in US equipment, including the F/A-18 Hornet and the JASSM long-range strike missile.[4]

Taken as a whole, Northern Europe and the US partnership with the countries of the region represent one of the unsung success stories of the post-Cold War era. As noted, Western democracies successfully shepherded northeastern Europe towards European and transatlantic integration, thereby advancing the US vision of a Europe whole, free and at peace. At the same time, as noted, the Nordic allies and partners became effective and sought-after participants in US-led expeditionary operations, whether in a NATO or coalition context.[5] For the US this was important beyond the actual forces contributed by the countries of Northern Europe. Individually and collectively, those states broadly share the traditional US view about the importance of maintaining a rules-based global order and advancing democracy, the rule of law and human rights. Having Northern Europe in Washington's corner therefore provide diplomatic benefits to US security-building.

---

[3] Nora Vanaga, 'Baltic Military Cooperation: Seeking a Common Response', Strategic Review No. 11, National Defence Academy of Latvia Center for Security and Strategic Research, April 2016, p. 1.

[4] See Charly Salonius-Pasternak, 'Not Just Another Arms Deal: The Security Policy Implications of the United States Selling Advanced Missiles to Finland', Finnish Institute of International Affairs (FIIA) Briefing Paper 112, September 2012.

[5] Ingrid Lundestad, 'Turning Security Importers to Exporters? US Strategy and Cooperation with Northern Europe Since 1993', *Journal of Transatlantic Studies* (Vol. 15, No. 3, 2017), pp. 251–72.

In spite of these successes, and the common values and worldview, Northern Europe presents complications when it comes to defence and security. First, the level of military capabilities and capacities varies markedly among the states of the region due to the different sizes of their economies. Second, investment in defence differs considerably, with the Baltic States at or near 2 per cent of GDP allocated to defence and Norway at 1.6 per cent, while others dedicate little more than 1 per cent.[6] While the proportion of GDP spent on defence is not necessarily directly relevant to measuring capabilities and capacities, it is of increasing interest in Washington at a time when Americans are increasingly concerned about burden-sharing. Third, cooperation across a range of areas has come relatively easily to the region, but has not necessarily been mirrored in defence and security. Northern European states have established various structures for regional cooperation over the years, including Nordic Defence Cooperation (NORDEFCO), Nordic–Baltic 8 (NB8) and the Northern Group led by the UK, but the results have so far been modest. Failures of several major joint-procurement projects have even led to controversy. Defence cooperation among the Baltic States, all of them NATO members, has achieved only mixed success. Finally, Northern Europe also consists of a patchwork of institutional affiliations, with many, but not all, states being members of the EU. With the exception of Sweden and Finland, all countries of Northern Europe are NATO members, with the other two close NATO partners.[7]

Northern Europe and the Return of Great-Power Competition

A new era of US engagement in Northern Europe began as Russia returned as a revanchist power. In the wake of the Ukraine crisis in 2014, US engagement in and with Northern Europe has changed considerably. Expeditionary operations are no longer the highest priority for US cooperation with the Norther European states, and the US now views the broader region as one of the zones of friction between NATO and a Putin intent on altering the European security order.

The administration of President Barack Obama took a series of measures to bolster deterrence in Northern Europe and to reassure NATO shortly after the Ukraine crisis began, which included rotating US forces into the region, upgrading and expanding infrastructure, and

---

[6] See NATO, 'Secretary General's Annual Report: The Alliance is Stepping Up', March 2018.

[7] See, for example, Heather A Conley, Jeffrey Rathke and Matthew Melino, *Enhanced Deterrence in the North: A 21st Century European Engagement Strategy* (Washington, DC: Center for Strategic and International Studies, 2018).

pre-positioning equipment. While President Donald Trump's administration has brought turbulence to the broader transatlantic relationship and uncertainty about the future of global US leadership, it is important to note that US defence engagement in Northern Europe has continued, and even intensified.

The Trump administration has significantly increased the funding available for the European Deterrence Initiative (EDI; previously called the European Reassurance Initiative by the Obama administration), which now stands at more than $4 billion. Much of this funding is intended to support exercises, the presence of US forces, and infrastructure improvement and expansion in Northern Europe from Lithuania to Iceland. Barring dramatic positive changes in the European security environment, EDI is likely to continue into the foreseeable future at current levels of funding. It will, however, constantly evolve and will increasingly incorporate air and maritime elements. Furthermore, while EDI to date has focused mainly on Europe's northeast, there is growing recognition in Washington that the Black Sea is also a zone of friction with Russia, and the region therefore merits greater US attention.

The US has also deployed high-end assets to Northern Europe for exercises, including B-52s, B-1s, B-2s, F-35s and Patriot air-defence batteries. Further, the US has deepened its defence relationships with a number of regional groupings, including US–UK–Norwegian cooperation on maritime patrol aircraft, and trilateral cooperation between the US, Sweden and Finland. In addition, US re-engagement in Northern Europe has produced a US return to Iceland, specifically the Keflavik airbase. The permanent US presence was withdrawn in 2006 as the US focused on counterinsurgency operations in the Middle East. The return to Keflavik by US Navy P-8s in 2017 on a rotational basis represents an important development given Iceland's strategic location in the far North Atlantic and the need to once again monitor and track the operations of Russia's Northern Fleet based on the Kola Peninsula.[8]

The Trump administration has also maintained the steady pace of visits to the region, with Secretary of Defense James Mattis visiting both Lithuania and Finland, and President Trump hosting the three Baltic presidents for a US–Baltic Summit on 3 April 2018. Key strategy documents released by the Trump administration, including both the National Security Strategy and the National Defense Strategy (NDS), identify a revisionist Russia, together with China, as strategic competitors of the US.

---

8 Nancy Montgomery, 'No Permanent Basing for Navy Sub Hunters in Iceland Despite Construction Projects', *Stars and Stripes*, 9 January 2018.

The NDS in particular de-emphasises counterterrorism and campaigning in the Middle East, the main preoccupation of US forces since the 9/11 attacks, in favour of posturing the US for a long-term contest with Russia and China and maintaining and extending the US military-technological edge. In addition, several key themes in the strategies have direct bearing on the security situation in Northern Europe, such as the attention paid to nuclear de-escalation and the deterrence of opportunist aggression. The NDS also prioritises enhancing and extending US alliances and partners, with NATO prominently featured.[9] US leadership within NATO has contributed further to a strengthened Alliance posture in Northern Europe, in particular with the Enhanced Forward Presence (EFP) battlegroups in Estonia, Latvia, Lithuania and Poland – multinational battalion-sized units led by the UK, Canada, Germany and the US.

While continued and even intensified US engagement in Northern Europe has done much to boost deterrence, the US, regional states and NATO still have considerable work to do. Two areas stand out in this regard: first, to create effective and robust reinforcement arrangements for the Baltic States to further bolster deterrence in peacetime and to increase the defensibility of northeastern Europe in wartime; and second, to return the focus of maritime operations to the North Atlantic to ensure that this maritime space will remain open for reinforcements from North America in case of crisis or war.[10]

These two key efforts involve more than just drawing up appropriate plans and dedicating resources. They also depend on building political will, both outside and within the context of NATO, as well as successfully fostering cooperative efforts among NATO members and between Alliance members and close partners.

The Way Forward

In light of the security and defence challenges in Northern Europe and the efforts made to date to bolster defence and deterrence, the US, NATO and the states of Northern Europe should consider these additional steps.

Command Structure Updates and Decision-Making

NATO must rapidly implement the adapted NATO command structure approved by defence ministers in early 2018, including the proposed new

---

[9] See Department of Defense, 'Summary of the 2018 National Defense Strategy of the United States of America: Sharpening the American Military's Competitive Edge', 2018, pp. 8–10.

[10] Franklin D Kramer and Hans Binnendijk, *Meeting the Russian Conventional Challenge* (Washington, DC: Atlantic Council, 2018).

Atlantic-focused Joint Forces Command (JFC) and the new logistics-focused Joint Support and Enabling Command (JSEC). The current JFC in Northern Europe – JFC Brunssum in the Netherlands – as well as NATO's Air Command in Germany and Maritime Command in the UK, must be bolstered with war-fighting capabilities and relevant regional expertise. In addition, NATO must fully integrate cyber elements into its commands at all levels, in coordination with the new Cyber Operations Centre at the Supreme Headquarters Allied Powers Europe (SHAPE) in Belgium. Perhaps most important, the NATO countries must commit themselves politically to provide full manning for the command structure to ensure it is at full readiness at all times.

NATO's decision-making is famously slow – the price of maintaining political consensus among 29 members. Still, NATO can take steps to speed up its reaction ahead of and during a crisis. For example, it could grant the Supreme Allied Commander Europe the authority to alert and stage forces without a North Atlantic Council (NAC) decision. NATO could also agree that all decisions deadlocked in the NAC must be raised with national capitals after 24 or 48 hours.

In addition, while NATO is and should remain the preferred vehicle for collective-defence and deterrence efforts, the North Atlantic Treaty does not prevent individual allies from deciding ahead of the Alliance as a whole to begin operations in defence of an ally. Informal coalitions of the willing should therefore be prepared to respond to a regional crisis in Northern Europe, in anticipation of eventual NATO action.

Readiness and Rapid Reinforcement

Real-world exercises, simulations and war-games have shown that Allied force readiness is woefully inadequate given the potential pace of events during a crisis in Northern Europe, especially one beginning with ambiguous 'hybrid' attacks. Therefore, the US needs to drive the effort to raise the readiness ('notice to move') of at least five Allied divisions to two weeks or less. This is necessary to provide back-up to the Very High Readiness Task Force ('Spearhead Force') and ensure reinforcements arrive rapidly enough to prevent the EFP from being overrun at the beginning of a conflict with Russia. The US should consider additional pre-positioning of armour and other equipment in the Baltic States and Poland to further speed up the reinforcement process.

Furthermore, NATO should create a mobility package (implemented in tandem with the EU) to address infrastructure gaps and bottlenecks and remove legal barriers to rapid movement across European national borders and from ports and airfields. NATO must also adequately exercise reinforcement efforts in both the Baltic Sea and North Atlantic regions to uncover further gaps and gain familiarity with terrain and host-nation conditions. These types of exercises would also signal to Russia NATO's enhanced capacity to reinforce and defend its members.

Enhancing Deterrence

The EFP battlegroups in Estonia, Latvia, Lithuania and Poland represent promising first steps toward building an Allied presence in NATO's front line states, and the participation of seventeen member states signals Allied commitment and solidarity. However, NATO must strengthen and complement the EFP battalions to bolster deterrence in Northern Europe even further. First, the Baltic Air Policing mission that has been underway since Estonia, Latvia and Lithuania joined the Alliance in 2004 should be transitioned to an air-defence capability. This would include an increased aviation presence in combination with ground-based air-defence assets supplied by the Baltic States, other NATO members, and the US.[11]

Russia depends on its growing network of air-defence and anti-ship missiles, along with ballistic missiles in the Kaliningrad exclave and the Kola Peninsula, to deny or impede US and NATO access to key parts of Northern Europe.[12] The US and NATO should consider counter-deployments of air and maritime assets to Northern Europe to demonstrate, for example, anti-submarine-warfare and long-range-strike capabilities, and to showcase the ability to effectively degrade Russian networks during a crisis.

The US should also consider deploying another Army Brigade Combat Team (ABCT) to Europe on a rotational basis. This would allow for regular deployments of US forces to the Baltic States in a coherent and sustained manner, as opposed to today's ad hoc approach. In addition, the US should expand the rotational presence of US Marine Corps forces in Norway, an initiative restarted in 2015 that not only sends a signal to Russia but also provides valuable training opportunities in a unique and challenging environment.

Over the last 30 years NATO has lost much of its instinct for high-end operations in the maritime domain due to its emphasis on ground-focused expeditionary operations. NATO must rectify this in light of Russia's growing naval power, especially the Northern Fleet, which constitutes a high concentration of combat power, including Russia's submarine-based

---

[11] Philip M Breedlove, 'Toward Effective Air Defense in Northern Europe', Atlantic Council, Scowcroft Center for Strategy and Security, February 2018.

[12] Guillaume Lasconjarias and Tomáš A Nagy, 'NATO Adaptation and A2/AD: Beyond Military Implications', GLOBSEC, 21 December 2017, <https://www.globsec.org/publications/nato-adaptation-a2ad-beyond-military-implications/>, accessed 20 July 2018.

nuclear deterrent, close to NATO territory. NATO should therefore update its Alliance Maritime Strategy and conduct additional exercises and deployments in the North Atlantic and the Baltic Sea.

Managing the Institutional Seams in Northern Europe

Sweden and Finland are both valued NATO partners that are also deepening their defence cooperation with the US and their neighbours. Due to their locations, they play vital roles in ensuring security in Northern Europe, particularly in the Baltic. However, they are not full members of NATO and therefore their security is not guaranteed under Article 5 of the North Atlantic Treaty. Thus, the roles of Sweden and Finland in both US and NATO strategy for defence against Russian aggression in the Baltic region will always have an element of ambiguity or uncertainty. The US and other NATO members will certainly seek and welcome Swedish and Finnish contributions of forces, access to airspace and waters, and intelligence sharing, but they cannot count on their availability in every contingency. Therefore, the US and its allies will always have to plan and ensure access to sufficient capabilities from other sources so that they are able to act without Sweden or Finland. Similarly, as non-members of NATO, Sweden and Finland are not obliged to contribute forces or support NATO even if invited to participate in planning and crisis consultations.

NATO can take measures to reduce this uncertainty and create a more coherent strategic space in Northern Europe. First, NATO could formalise existing 29 + 2 mechanisms as a Baltic Security Commission (BSC), similar to the NATO–Georgia or NATO–Ukraine commissions, with a regular rhythm of political consultations and activities, including joint threat assessments, information sharing and contingency planning, as well as exercises and simulations. Should a crisis emerge in the Baltic, the BSC could become the principal forum for consultations and decision-making on ways to prevent or de-escalate the crisis, as well as on strategic messaging towards Russia.

Second, Sweden and Finland should consider contributing forces to one or more of the EFP battalions in the Baltic States, including staff officers, thus becoming more integrally involved in crisis-planning and operations. Short of that, they could exercise on a periodic basis with the EFP battalions and with the US rotational ABCT. Sweden and Finland could assign liaison officers to JFC Brunssum, and NATO in turn could assign liaison officers to the Swedish and Finnish national military commands to ensure greater synchronisation of planning and to promote greater mutual understanding of each side's priorities and *modus operandi* in a crisis.

Integrating NATO, Swedish and Finnish efforts in contingency planning along these lines, and operating together or in close coordination in Northern Europe on a more systematic basis, would yield several benefits. These include augmenting NATO's military strength, increasing political solidarity, and providing additional flexibility to the US and other allies in allocating capabilities to counter Russian threats. Deterrence of Russia would increase to the extent Moscow perceives Sweden and Finland as adding forces or strategic depth to the Alliance, and if NATO and Sweden and Finland were coordinating their strategic communications.

Conclusion

Northern Europe is central to the competition between the West and Russia over the future of the European security order and, by extension, of the rules-based global order. The US, regional states and NATO are all adapting to this new reality, but must still address urgent issues to provide for effective deterrence and robust defence. Continued US leadership is crucial in forging bilateral and multilateral cooperation in the region, as well as within NATO, to build capabilities and ensure an adequate US presence. At the same time, appropriate burden-sharing among the US, its allies in Northern Europe, and the rest of NATO has never been more important. This is due not only to domestic political uncertainties in the US, but also to the turbulent global security environment, with potential crises in Asia and the Middle East forcing the US to balance its commitments and attention across multiple regions and continents.

Some Northern European states must assume more of the shared defence burden. Defence experts and officials in Washington certainly understand the nuances of measuring inputs and outputs in defence, and realise that many Northern European defence establishments are skilled at producing maximum capacity and capability with limited resources. They also recognise that the 2 per cent commitment within NATO is an imperfect yardstick. However, Trump has changed the parameters of this debate in Washington, and US policy circles now closely track and comment on European defence spending. The 2 per cent commitment may say very little about defence capacities and capabilities, but in Washington's eyes it says a great deal about the political commitment each ally dedicates to the transatlantic Alliance.

US engagement in and with Northern Europe, inside and outside NATO, has advanced significantly over the last four years. It provides a solid base for the work that remains to be done to bolster deterrence against a newly aggressive Russia and to forge closer integration among allies and partners in the region. As the broader Northern European region has become a focal point for the contest between NATO and Russia over the future of the European security order, the relationship between the US and Northern Europe has never been more important, or a common agenda more urgent.

IX. CANADA AND SECURITY IN NORTHERN EUROPE

DAVID PERRY

Canada's post-war international policy has been deeply shaped by atlanticism – a multi-faceted connection to NATO. The Alliance has, of course, afforded Canada core protections and these considerations have driven much of Canada's connection with NATO. However, Canada's fondness for the Alliance goes beyond purely defensive concerns; other elements have sustained Canadian support for NATO even when hard-security concerns have waned and Canada's views have diverged from those of its allies. Key among these softer ties, the Alliance also represents a 'community of shared values' created by transatlantic familial relations, cultural ties and trade with Europe – especially with the UK and France, Canada's two foundational linguistic communities.[1]

Beyond this, NATO has offered Canada 'a seat at the most important allied table in the world'[2] and a strong voice in the world's foremost multilateral defence forum. In doing so, NATO has provided Canada with a European counterweight to US security interests, somewhat moderating the US's otherwise dominant voice in Canadian defence and security discussions.[3] Thus, while hard-security concerns drove Canada's involvement in the creation of and continued participation in NATO during the Cold War, these other benefits helped sustain Canada's strong

---

[1] David Pratt, 'Canadian Grand Strategy and Lessons Learned', *Journal of Transatlantic Studies* (Vol. 6, No. 1, 2008), p. 63.

[2] Kim Richard Nossal, 'A European Nation? The Life and Times of Atlanticism in Canada', in John English and Norman Hillmer (eds), *Making a Difference?* (Toronto: Lester Publishing Limited, 1992), p. 316.

[3] Robert Bothwell, 'Serial Monogamy or Constructive Bigamy', in Greg Anderson and Christopher Sands (eds), *Forgotten Partnership Redux* (Amherst, NY: Cambria Press, 2011), pp. 15–30.

support for the Alliance even after the Soviet threat disappeared. This dual focus on hard security and softer benefits serves as an important context to understand how Canada's relationship with the Alliance has evolved over time, even as core security considerations have waned. It explains how Canada has remained an enthusiastic contributor to reassurance and deterrence initiatives in Europe since 2014, despite views about Russia that diverge from some allies.

From the North Atlantic Treaty to Crimea

NATO considerations drove much Canadian post-war defence planning, starting with a rearmament programme after a significant post-war demobilisation. Although the build-up began in response to the Korean War, once troops were deployed to that theatre efforts were re-oriented around defending NATO Europe.[4] Beginning in 1951, the Canadian Army deployed 6,000 troops to Germany; the Royal Canadian Air Force (RCAF) sent twelve squadrons and 300 aircraft; while the Royal Canadian Navy (RCN) eventually contributed a fleet of 50 vessels, including submarines and an aircraft carrier, to the defence of the North Atlantic.[5]

Although Canadian peacekeeping efforts often receive greater place of pride in Canada's public consciousness, the preponderance of Canadian military activity during the Cold War centred on NATO duties.[6] For much of the 1950s and 1960s, Canada had 12,000 troops stationed in Europe – commitments so extensive that by the early 1970s some argued Canadian defence policy amounted to little more than the sum total of Canada's NATO commitments.[7] Concern about the disproportionate focus on Alliance concerns drove then Prime Minister Pierre Trudeau's first government to re-evaluate Canadian NATO policy, reducing the army's contribution to 2,800 troops and the RCAF's to three squadrons, for a total of 5,000 troops.[8] Yet, despite initial antipathy towards the Alliance, Trudeau created a Canadian Air-Sea Transportable Brigade, based in Canada but intended for deployment to NATO's northern flank in Norway, in a move designed to offset the impact of the reduction in Canadian troops permanently stationed in Europe. Further, when he reviewed Canadian defence policy in 1974–75 he recommitted to the

---

4 David Bercuson, *True Patriot* (Toronto: University of Toronto Press, 1993).

5 Joseph T Jockel and Joel J Sokolsky, 'Canada and NATO', *International Journal* (Vol. 64, No. 2, 2009), pp. 315–36.

6 Sean M Maloney, *War Without Battles* (Whitby, ON: McGraw-Hill Ryerson, 1996).

7 Douglas Bland, 'A Sow's Ear from a Silk Purse', *International Journal* (Vol. 54, No. 1, 1998–99), pp. 143–74.

8 J L Granatstein and Robert Bothwell, *Pirouette* (Toronto: University of Toronto Press, 1990).

Alliance, initiating a programme of military investment to allow Canada to honour its NATO obligations. This recommitment was partly driven by a desire to establish stronger economic ties with Western Europe, exemplified by the purchase of Leopard tanks from West Germany in part for access to trade, highlighting the importance of non-security ties in Canada's links with NATO Europe.[9]

The end of the Cold War coincided with Canada's embrace of fiscal discipline and decreases in defence budgets made a significant contribution to government-wide spending reductions that started in 1989. Over the following decade cuts were apportioned across the Canadian military, reducing troop strength, curtailing procurement, and closing bases, including Canada's European installations in 1992. In the wake of these closures, with the Alliance's traditional collective defence role waning and NATO's focus shifting towards a crisis-management role in the Balkans, some understandably expressed concerns that Canada's support for NATO would wither.[10] Between 1989 and 1999, the share of Canada's GDP devoted to defence dropped from 2 per cent in 1990 to 1.2 per cent by 2000, a level at which it remained until 2006.[11] The size of the armed forces decreased considerably over this period.

Along with smaller overall budgets, the portion of the Canadian defence budget devoted to equipment investment and research and development fell below 15 per cent after 1996 and has remained below this level. This was a consequence of anaemic capital investment; for example, from the end of the Cold War through the mid-2000s, only the army's Light Armoured Vehicle fleet and the RCN's submarines were replaced (the latter with second-hand boats). The military initiated major life extensions and mid-life upgrades, rather than replacement projects, for RCAF aircraft and RCN frigates; consequently, by the mid-2000s Canada's equipment base was rapidly rusting out.[12]

Starting in 2007, following the publication by both of Canada's main political parties of successive defence policies predicated on military investment, the share of Canada's GDP devoted to defence increased for a

---

[9] Peter Haydon and Dan Middlemiss, 'The 1975 Defence Structure Review', in Yves Tremblay (ed.), *Canadian Military History Since the 17th Century* (Ottawa: Directorate of History, DND, 2001).

[10] Paul Buteux, Michel Fortman and Pierre Martin, 'Canada and the Expansion of NATO', in David G Haglund (ed.), *Will NATO Go East?* (Kingston: Centre for International Relations, Queen's University, 1996), pp. 147–79.

[11] NATO, 'Information on Defence Expenditures (Various Years)', <https://www.nato.int/cps/ic/natohq/topics_49198.htm>, accessed 20 July 2018.

[12] Brian MacDonald, 'The Capital and the Future Force Crisis', in Douglas L Bland (ed.) *Canada Without Armed Forces* (Montreal: McGill-Queen's University Press, 2004), pp. 24–54.

few years. These additional funds supported an expansion of the military and a number of major equipment purchases. Much of this effort was directed towards properly equipping Canada's Afghan operations as the army replaced its combat vehicles and acquired counterinsurgency-specific equipment, and the RCAF obtained new transport fleets to support the war effort. Closer to home, a defence policy focused on enhancing Canadian sovereign presence at home resulted in projects to provide the RCN with its first purpose-built Arctic vessels in 50 years and a refuelling station in the eastern Arctic.

After 2010, however, the share of GDP devoted to defence again started to decline and the rate of new procurement slowed once the government enacted deficit-reduction measures. During this period of divestment, the Canadian military withdrew its participation in NATO's AWACS programme, the Alliance Ground Surveillance system. In the context of major budget pressures, the decision resulted from Canadian frustration with the Alliance's inability to have common-funded programmes such as AWACS support in out-of-area operations in Afghanistan and Libya.[13]

Despite reduced investment and changed strategic circumstances, the fear that Canada would reduce its engagement in NATO after the Cold War proved unfounded. A desire to support the Alliance in its new crisis-management role, rather than any particular concern for Balkan security, drove a Canadian contribution of thousands of troops over several years, reaching a peak of 4,000 personnel.[14] Thus, Canada remained a 'committed, capable and dedicated ally,'[15] willing to shoulder a proportional role in NATO crisis response. This was also true in Afghanistan where, in addition to supporting the US, Canada's largest foreign deployment since the Korean War was also a pledge of 'solidarity within the alliance'.[16] Subsequent participation in operations in Libya, where Canada contributed the leadership element, refuelling, and fighter and surveillance aircraft, as well as a frigate, also reaffirmed the importance of NATO to Canada's foreign policy.

---

[13] David Perry, *Doing Less with Less* (Ottawa: Conference of Defence Associations, 2014).

[14] Some have argued that Canadian participation in UN missions in the Balkans in the early 1990s, prior to joining NATO's operations there, was driven by a desire to restore relations with NATO Europe following the withdrawal of Canada's troops from Europe, as much as any desire to engage in UN operations. See Sean Maloney, 'Helpful Fixer, or Hired Gun? Why Canada Goes Overseas', *Policy Options*, 1 January 2001.

[15] Benjamin Zyla, 'Years of Free-Riding?', *American Review of Canadian Studies* (Vol. 40, No. 1, 2010), p. 23.

[16] David McDonough, 'Afghanistan and Renewing Canadian Leadership', *International Journal* (Vol. 64, No. 3, 2009), p. 648.

As these historical examples indicate, when a strategic threat to NATO collective defence existed, Canada contributed directly to European security. When this threat waned, it did little to reduce Canada's commitment to the Alliance; it just changed the focus of that support to participation in crisis-management operations. This waning threat coincided with a sharp reduction in Canadian defence spending and investment, so Canadian governments preferred that their contribution to the Alliance be measured by actions, not dollars. This mindset still holds, as Canadian officials continue to note that Canada has participated in every NATO 'mission, operation, and activity' since its foundation.[17]

From Crimea to the Present

The focus of Canada's relationship with NATO changed once again after Russia's 2014 annexation of Crimea and subsequent campaign in Eastern Ukraine. While an enthusiastic supporter of NATO crisis-response measures, Canada had no troop presence in Europe, so re-engagement in Alliance collective defence has driven a considerable change in Canadian force posture, with Canada participating in a series of continuous expeditionary operations to deploy troops to Europe to provide a sustained presence on the continent.

In response to the Russian action in Crimea, Canada immediately moved to impose sanctions against Russian officials and curtail diplomatic engagement, end military cooperation and recall Canada's ambassador from Moscow. Simultaneously, then Prime Minister Stephen Harper was the first G7 leader to visit the new Ukrainian government in Kiev. Then, starting in April 2014, Canada launched Operation *Reassurance*, which has seen thousands of troops rotate through European deployments.[18] At the same time, Canada has embarked on a series of measures to show support for the government of Ukraine, including military training in western Ukraine, and considers these measures as part of its wider support for NATO.[19]

In April 2014, Canada deployed an air task force to Romania to conduct air policing, and the same month a Canadian frigate, HMCS

---

[17] House of Commons Chambre des Communes, 'Evidence', Standing Committee on National Defence, Number 79, 1st Session, 42nd Parliament, 6 February 2018, Kerry Buck, p. 7, <http://www.ourcommons.ca/DocumentViewer/en/42-1/NDDN/meeting-79/evidence>, accessed 20 July 2018.

[18] National Defence and the Canadian Armed Forces, 'Operation REASSURANCE', 2018, <http://www.forces.gc.ca/en/operations-abroad/nato-ee.page>, accessed 20 July 2018.

[19] Andrew Rasiulius, 'Canada's Military Operations on NATO's Eastern Flank', *Global Exchange* (Vol. 16, No. 4, Fall 2017), pp. 27–29.

Regina, was re-tasked to participate in NATO reassurance measures. Additional fighter aircraft were deployed to Lithuania to conduct Baltic air policing at the end of 2014. In June 2017, Canada deployed aircraft to Iceland to conduct a NATO surveillance and intercept mission, and in September of the same year deployed another fighter contingent to Romania to conduct an air-policing mission. At sea, HMCS *Regina* has been replaced by a series of Canadian frigates, largely deployed under one of NATO's Standing Maritime Groups. This has effectively kept a Canadian frigate continuously deployed as part of NATO reassurance measures since spring 2014. Finally, since May 2014 the Canadian Army has rotated numerous units, up to company size, through training exercises in Poland, Latvia, Germany, Lithuania, Estonia, Romania, Hungary and Bulgaria.[20]

These reassurance measures have spanned two governments with substantially different approaches to foreign relations. In its 2015 election platform, the Liberal Party of Canada, led by Justin Trudeau, proposed significant changes from the Harper government's international policies, pledging to put Canada 'back' on the international stage. With regard to defence specifically, the Liberals promised to withdraw fighter jets from operations in the Middle East and vowed not to purchase the F-35. These moves were driven by political rather than strategic considerations, but demonstrated the party's appetite for a new approach to defence issues. However, the Liberal Party pledged to remain 'fully committed'[21] to Canada's NATO reassurance missions and has remained so since taking office.

When combined with ongoing efforts in the air and at sea, Operation *Reassurance* collectively represents Canada's largest deployment abroad. At the 2016 NATO Summit in Warsaw, the first after Justin Trudeau's election, Canada announced it would lead the Latvian battlegroup, becoming one of the four framework nations under NATO's Enhanced Forward Presence (EFP) in Eastern Europe.[22] Canada has contributed up to 450 troops to this mission, including the headquarters element, a mechanised-infantry company, combat-service support, and vehicles and equipment.[23] By Canadian standards, this mission is large, especially in the context of a

---

20 National Defence and the Canadian Armed Forces, 'Operation REASSURANCE'.

21 Liberal Party of Canada, *A New Plan for a Strong Middle Class* (Ottawa: Liberal Party of Canada, 2015).

22 National Defence and the Canadian Armed Forces, 'Operation REASSURANCE'.

23 Justin Trudeau, Prime Minister of Canada, 'Canada Makes Commitment to NATO Defence and Deterrence Measures', 8 July 2016, <https://pm.gc.ca/eng/news/2016/07/08/canada-makes-commitment-nato-defence-and-deterrence-measures>, accessed 20 July 2018.

concurrent deployment of 600–800 troops to the Middle East and Trudeau's pledged re-engagement in UN peacekeeping.[24] Furthermore, its leadership role in an operation in close proximity to Russia represents the first 'persistent Canadian military presence in Europe'[25] since Canada withdrew its forces in the 1990s. As with Balkan operations during that decade, the Latvian deployment represents primarily an expression of support for NATO's collective defence and an indication that Article 5 remains at the heart of Canadian national security policy, rather than concern for the Baltic States generally or Latvia specifically.[26]

While strongly supportive of Alliance deterrence efforts in Europe, Canada's policy towards Russia has been more complicated than its support for NATO would otherwise suggest. Canadian analysts have followed Russia's significant military modernisation since the mid-2000s, initially assessing it as 'intended for territorial security, commercial development and search and rescue'.[27] But Russia's military activities in its Arctic territory are of special concern to Canada. First, as indicated above, Canadian officials have described this modernisation as enhancing Russia's ability to act in its own Arctic territory. Second, because most Russian strategic capability is located in its Arctic territory, they have acknowledged that it represents a major upgrade of Russia's globally deployable strategic forces, which while based in the Russian Arctic can be employed anywhere in the world.[28] This has been brought home to Canada by Russia's resumption of long-range air patrols near the Canadian Arctic Archipelago and the coastal approaches to North America since the late 2000s. After Canada began its NATO reassurance measures and support for Ukraine, some of these flights have coincided with visits by Ukrainian officials to Canada in what appears to have been strategic signalling of Russian displeasure.[29]

---

[24] This was the size of Canada's Middle East mission at the time the Latvian deployment was announced; troop numbers in the Middle East have since declined. As of March 2018, Canada has yet to follow through on this deployment.
[25] House of Commons Chambre des Communes, 'Evidence', Marquise Hainse, p. 3.
[26] Alexander Lanoszka, 'From Ottawa to Riga', *International Journal* (Vol. 72, No. 4, 2017), pp. 520–37.
[27] David Rudd, 'The Russian Federation Navy Post-2015', *Canadian Naval Review* (Vol. 11, No. 1, Spring 2015), p. 8.
[28] House of Commons Chambre des Communes, 'Evidence', Standing Committee on National Defence, Number 26, 1st Session, 42nd Parliament, 3 November 2016, Stephen Burt, p. 5.
[29] Steven Chase, 'Russian Military Jets Flew Within 100 Kilometres of Canadian Mainland', *Globe and Mail*, 19 September 2014, <https://www.theglobeandmail.com/news/politics/russian-military-jets-flew-within-100-kilometres-of-canadian-mainland-source-says/article20706528/>, accessed 7 April 2018.

Since Crimea, Canadian officials have characterised Russia's modernised capabilities, their use in Crimea, and Russia's resumption of out-of-area military activity at levels not seen since the collapse of the Soviet Union as a challenge to the rules-based international order and a threat to international security. Trudeau's second foreign minister, Chrystia Freeland, has pointedly described Russia's destabilising activities abroad as representing a strategic threat to the liberal-democratic world.[30] Yet, when discussing Canadian security and defence in conjunction with Russia, Canadian officials have been remarkably circumspect and instead go to great pains to state that Russia poses no threat to Canada, as they see no Russian malign intent accompanying the improvements in capability,[31] and characterise Russia's actions towards Canada as totally different from its activities beyond Canada's borders. Regarding Canada's Arctic territory in particular, Canadian officials continue to state that they see no 'active military threat in our own Arctic' and furthermore that the Canadian Arctic is 'an area of cooperation'.[32]

This seemingly contradictory assessment of Russia as a strategic threat that must be deterred on Europe's east, but a benign actor in Canada's north, would seem to reflect the Trudeau government's two-pronged approach towards Russia. Having campaigned on a promise to end the Harper government's 'empty chair'[33] policy of diplomatic non-engagement with Russia, the current government has pursued a twin-track policy involving both dialogue with Russia and deterrence of it. Trudeau's first foreign minister, Stéphane Dion, vigorously embraced renewing relations with Russia and put particular focus on the Arctic. During his tenure, which ended in January 2017, re-engagement with Russia received greater prominence in public statements than deterrence or reassurance measures.[34]

The view that Canada should engage with Russia regarding the Arctic has persisted even after Russia's Syria intervention that began in autumn 2015. The showcasing of Russia's new precision-guided, manoeuvrable and stealthy conventional cruise missiles present particular dilemmas for Canada in the context of North American defence. The existing defence networks that Canada shares with the US are not suited to protect against

---

[30] Chrystia Freeland, 'Chrystia Freeland on Canada's Foreign Policy: Full Speech', 6 June 2017.

[31] House of Commons Chambre des Communes, 'Evidence', Stephen Burt, p. 5.

[32] *Ibid.*, Kerry Buck, p. 10.

[33] Stéphane Dion, 'On "Responsible Conviction" and Liberal Foreign Policy', *Maclean's*, 29 March 2016.

[34] House of Commons Chambre des Communes, 'Evidence', Standing Committee on Foreign Affairs and International Development, Number 7, 1st Session, 42nd Parliament,14 April 2016, Stéphane Dion.

these new classes of missile, which can be launched from aircraft, submarines or surface ships at stand-off range from North American territory and strike targets inland. NORAD, the binational defence command for North America, has concluded that Russia's actions in both Eastern Europe and the Middle East signal sufficient antagonistic intent and demonstrated capabilities to justify an assessment that Russia presents a threat to North America.[35] Notably, Canadian officers working for NORAD (and therefore reporting to the American commander) have made public comments echoing NORAD's language and repeated the assessment that Russia presents a threat, but they remain the only Canadians to do so openly.

Canada's convoluted stance towards Russia has complicated the nation's support for collective defence through NATO and created a curious dynamic. Canadian actions and policies designed to either deter or bolster defences against a resurgent Russia have been more coherent and consistent the further away from Canadian territory they are applied. As evidenced by its willingness to lead NATO's Latvian battlegroup, Canada has been more publicly supportive of NATO efforts to deter and counter Russia on Europe's northeastern flank than in Canada's own north. Furthermore, until the publication of the 2017 defence policy, Canada had opposed efforts to involve NATO in Canada's Arctic and objected to NATO discussions of the Arctic generally.[36]

The Future: Northern Security Under the 2017 Defence Policy

Canada's strong support for the security of northern Europe and NATO's collective defence is unlikely to change. In June 2017 Canada published its first defence policy since 2008, entitled *Strong, Secure, Engaged*, outlining a twenty-year vision for Canada's defence.[37] Canada's long-term plan for military investment indicates that this vision will be backed by increased military capacity. The new defence policy, and the foreign policy direction that preceded it, also indicate a clearer-eyed view of Russia than the Trudeau government initially demonstrated. But as the Alliance shifts its focus increasingly northward, the tension between Canada's readiness to support NATO and counter Russian aggression in northeastern Europe on the one hand, and its more nuanced views about Russia in the Arctic on the other, will likely grow.

---

35 NORAD officials, comments to academic study tour, Colorado Springs, March 2016.

36 Yves Brodeur, 'NATO', *Global Exchange* (Vol. 16, No. 4, Fall 2017), pp. 16–18.

37 National Defence, *Strong, Secure, Engaged: Canada's Defence Policy* (Ottawa: Minister of National Defence, 2017).

The most recent formal articulation of Canadian foreign policy holds that the North Atlantic Alliance remains the 'cornerstone'[38] of Canada's multilateral approach to international affairs and one of the key guarantors of the liberal international order that Canada deeply values. Given the increased uncertainty about the willingness of the US under President Trump to continue its role as a global defence and security leader and the turmoil surrounding his administration, NATO's relative status within Canadian international policy has only grown. With America ambivalent about the post-war international order it constructed, NATO's value as a guarantor of Canadian security, counterweight to Washington, and reinforcement of the international status quo has increased. Canada's ambassador to NATO has characterised Alliance unity as the 'strongest deterrent to aggression',[39] which indicates that Canada will orient its NATO policy around a desire to support the Alliance itself. As in the past, Canada's future approach to security in Northern Europe will focus on support for NATO as an institution more than on the advancement of any particular strategic objective.

Strong, Secure, Engaged is not truly a strategic document, as it does not provide an explicit articulation of defence priorities. It does, however, acknowledge a number of changes to the international environment, alter Canada's proposed operational employment model, and propose meaningful future investments in defence capability, all of which will positively affect Canada's ability to support the security of Northern Europe. The policy recognises that 'a degree of major power competition has returned to the international system',[40] with particular emphasis on Russia. As a result, it has reintroduced 'strategic deterrence' into the Canadian defence lexicon for the first time in 30 years. Specifically, it acknowledges that Canada benefits from NATO deterrence and that Canada must contribute to these efforts in all domains. *Strong, Secure, Engaged* further calls for Canada to remain a 'responsible partner'[41] that adds value to its traditional alliances and NATO specifically, and emphasises that Canadian planning and capability development must prioritise interoperability with NATO.[42] To do so, Canada must maintain 'high-quality, interoperable, and expeditionary forces which Canada can deploy, as needed, to effectively contribute to NATO's deterrence posture, operations, exercises, and capacity building activities'.[43]

---

38 Freeland, 'Chrystia Freeland on Canada's Foreign Policy: Full Speech'.
39 House of Commons Chambre des Communes, 'Evidence', Kerry Buck, p. 11.
40 National Defence, *Strong, Secure, Engaged*, p. 50.
41 *Ibid.*, p. 57.
42 *Ibid.*, p. 61.
43 *Ibid.*, p. 91.

Even so, Canada's conflicted defence views of the Arctic remain evident in this new policy. In the section on global context, the discussion of the Arctic focuses only on increased civilian accessibility of the region due to the impact of climate change and improved technology. Consequently, the suggested military posture for the Arctic in this area of the policy is limited to an increase in constabulary response. Yet the document later proposes multiple enhancements to Canada's core Arctic military capability, many specifically to contribute to the defence of North America. These enhancements include modernisation of the North Warning System early-warning radar; intelligence, surveillance and reconnaissance and space-based communications; and enhancements to northern logistical arrangements, including the Forward Operating Locations for the RCAF.

In addition to recognising the need to invest with the US in the Arctic aspects of North American defence, the new policy also recognises the growing importance of the Arctic to NATO. It acknowledges the increased attention the Alliance has paid to Russia's ability to project forces from its own Arctic territory and the challenge those forces present to NATO's collective-defence posture. In a significant change to Canadian policy, *Strong, Secure, Engaged* directs that Canada will 'conduct joint exercises with Arctic allies and partners and support the strengthening of situational awareness and information sharing in the Arctic, including with NATO'.[44] The inclusion of the words 'Arctic' and 'NATO' in the same sentence in and of itself symbolises an important change in Canadian policy, as does the actual initiative. Yet in the months since publication, Canadian diplomats have continued to assert that Russia poses no threat in Canada's Arctic, which remains a zone for cooperation.[45]

More positively, for the first time Canadian defence policy has directed the military to be able to conduct the full suite of operations concurrently. Previous policies had never established what the government expected the military to do at any given time, leaving precise force-structure requirements uncertain and Canada unable to conduct all of the operations committed to in formal policy simultaneously. The new policy specifies that the Canadian military must be able to meet its commitments to NATO under Article 5 of the North Atlantic Treaty at the same time as those to NORAD and to any other envisioned deployment. Once the force structure and readiness changes required to enact this change are in place, Canadian commitments to Alliance collective defence will become more credible.

---

44 *Ibid.*, p. 80.

45 House of Commons Chambre des Communes, 'Evidence', Kerry Buck, p. 10.

The policy furthermore calls for significant defence investment. An additional $62.3 billion in new spending over 20 years would be added to prior defence plans, of which approximately three-quarters would go towards investment in capital equipment and new infrastructure. After decades of underinvestment, the new funding will allow 52 new major projects to go forward, replacing existing capabilities and adding investment in critical areas such as C4ISR and cyber capabilities. Further, the policy and its supporting funding base have added tens of billions of dollars to the budgets of projects to upgrade Canada's air and naval combat fleets. This will allow a one-for-one replacement of the RCN's surface-combatant fleet and facilitate a modest growth in the size of Canada's fighter fleet from 76 to 88 jets. The increased size of Canada's fighter capability is a direct outcome of the Trudeau government's policy direction that in the future, the RCAF must be able to meet Canada's NORAD and NATO air commitments concurrently, which will significantly increase the future credibility of Canada's latter commitment.

The additional spending outlined in *Strong, Secure, Engaged* will push Canadian defence spending up to 1.4 per cent of GDP as a result of both actual increases and a recalculation of how Canada reports its spending to NATO, which has added another 0.2 per cent to previously reported figures.[46] This spending increase would also increase the proportion allocated to equipment investment to 32 per cent of defence expenditure within six years. To actually increase expenditure on equipment as much and as quickly as intended is already proving difficult, but if the intent outlined in *Strong, Secure, Engaged* is realised, it will reverse the decline in the share of GDP Canada devotes to defence and significantly boost spending on equipment investment.[47] Although the policy officially shows that Canada has no intention of ever meeting NATO's target of spending 2 per cent of GDP on defence, it indicates Canada's intention to meet and then significantly exceed the Alliance's target of allocating 20 per cent of defence expenditure to equipment investment. This will provide a major boost to core military capabilities, providing Canada with an enhanced ability to support collective defence efforts in Europe.

Conclusion

Through NATO, Canada is a strong supporter of the security of Northern Europe due to its concern for collective defence and links with Europe.

[46] National Defence, *Strong, Secure, Engaged*, p. 46. The amounts vary year by year but the average over the ten-year period depicted in the policy is 0.2 per cent of GDP.

[47] David Perry, *Following the Funding in Strong, Secure, Engaged* (Calgary: Canadian Global Affairs Institute, 2018).

While the government's views have evolved over time, current Canadian support for Alliance reassurance and deterrence measures is firm. Looking to the future, if Canada realises the vision in its new defence policy, it will remain a committed NATO member with investments that enhance its ability to share the collective-defence burden and contribute militarily towards defence and security in Northern Europe. At the same time, Canada's view that Russia presents a strategic threat abroad, yet no threat to Canada's Arctic, may represent the lone point of contention with NATO as the Alliance turns its focus further northward to provide for collective defence. Even if the Alliance's northern focus remains east of Greenland, an increased NATO focus on the Arctic will be uncomfortable for Canada to rationalise with its unique views of its security situation in the Canadian north.

X. NATO AND THE CHALLENGE IN THE NORTH ATLANTIC AND THE ARCTIC

JAMES G FOGGO AND ALARIK FRITZ

It has been said far too often that 'the world changed on 9/11'. Since that day, most Americans have seen the challenges of the world revolving around terrorism and ongoing conflicts in the Middle East. Similarly, since the end of the Cold War, NATO has focused largely on crisis management and counterinsurgency, especially on the southern flank. The instability created by violent-extremist organisations is a clear and present threat, and NATO is helping to address it in a variety of non-kinetic ways. NATO is meeting the problems that come with ungoverned spaces, a declining rule of law, narcotics, and weapons and human trafficking head on. The Alliance recognises these as fundamental challenges that it must and will continue to deal with. However, we also need to recall those challenges that did not change on 9/11: namely, those associated with the security of the North Atlantic.

We cannot predict with certainty where the next threat will emerge, or where the next war will take place – but the security of the North Atlantic has always been a focal point for NATO. Today's Allies operated in this environment through two world wars and the entire Cold War for a very good reason: this is where a single miscalculation could have erupted into a global nuclear conflict. The North Atlantic remains absolutely critical to the West's collective security. The unavoidable operational reality is that should conflict arise, whoever can exert control over this region can either protect or threaten all of NATO's northern flank. Defence of the North Atlantic is thus synonymous with Alliance security and sovereignty. In the post-9/11 and post-Cold War era, we need to remember this and ensure that these enduring truths are fully embodied in NATO members states' national security policies, strategies and force deployments.

To ensure a peaceful and prosperous Europe and North America, NATO needs to be ready for any contingency. It has to be able to maintain regional stability on its flanks, prevent crises or small wars from erupting or spreading and, at the same time, still deter potential threats to our security as a collective. The ready and postured forces of member states, enabled by their mutual commitment, are what empower NATO to do all of these things. With this in mind, in this chapter we will outline the potential challenges that NATO faces in the North Atlantic today, how NATO is meeting them, and how it must continue to do so.

What are the Challenges?

The one constant that must guide NATO policies, operations and forces is that, regardless of whatever regional challenges it is addressing, it must also be prepared to deter the most capable adversary it might face. Today, that is Russia. Of course, this does not mean that such a conflict is likely. Our hope has always been that Russia will be fully and peacefully integrated into the rules-based and prosperous global system established after the Second World War. But Russia has acted aggressively in the European theatre and has demonstrated its willingness to interfere in the political and economic affairs of sovereign states. When we examine the strategic laydown of forces across the theatre, it is clear that the greatest potential challenge to NATO security today comes from Russia, much as it did from the USSR during the Cold War. NATO operational forces, as the guarantors of their individual states' sovereignty, must be prepared to face any such threats. That is why maintaining deterrent capability, and thereby ensuring peace in Europe, remains a top priority for US European Command.

Much has changed in Europe since the end of the Cold War. During one of the authors' first deployments to the Baltic Sea in 1985 – then as Lieutenant Foggo aboard USS *Sea Devil* – many Warsaw Pact vessels surveyed or harassed the submarine on an inbound transit to Kiel. Those Warsaw Pact states are now full members of NATO and some of our staunchest allies. But other changes include a radically different and aggressive Russian military. To ensure our security into the future, we must make sure that we adapt our operations, policies and forces to any and all such changes.

During the Cold War, US policy towards the USSR focused entirely on containment, and both sides endeavoured to avoid conflict lest they slide into nuclear confrontation. However, Russian actions in the past decade make it clear that they are focused on conflict escalation. Invading

Georgia, illegally annexing Crimea, inciting tensions with the Baltic States, active military operations and long-range strikes into Syria, and dangerous incidents and fly-bys at sea have all been increasingly oriented towards challenging us in unpredictable ways. Russia clearly places more importance on escalation dominance than escalation avoidance. This means that we need to be even more capable, postured and ready so that we can maintain deterrence and mitigate any risks of operational brinksmanship.

Furthermore, Russia has intentionally and cleverly renewed its capabilities in the North Atlantic and the Arctic in places not seen since the Cold War. For example, Russian forces have recently reoccupied seven of their former Soviet Union bases in the Arctic Circle. This improves Russia's capability to project power into the crucial strategic routes from the Arctic into the North Atlantic and the Greenland–Iceland–UK (GIUK) gap. This does not have to be an alarming development. In fact, US Navy forces operate north of the Arctic Circle as well, to ensure the security of commerce and demonstrate freedom of navigation in that complex environment. Nonetheless, this apparent militarisation of the Arctic by Russia risks destabilising the region. Heretofore, this region has seen extensive and peaceful economic cooperation between Russia and its neighbours. Now, however, it appears that Russia is moving towards considering the Arctic to be its own territory – to the extent that Russian forces have even planted a Russian flag on the sea floor at the geographic North Pole.

At the same time, Russian naval forces are in the middle of a massive and historic transition to a smaller but much higher-quality professional force, more capable and lethal than ever before. This changing force is complemented by a series of interlocking coastal defence missiles, land-based aircraft and air-defence systems. As a result, Russia now has counter-power-projection bastions from which its forces can operate in an attempt to threaten North Atlantic sea lines of communication and populations, unless we prevent them from doing so. Russia has also reinvigorated its ability to conduct meaningful out-of-area power projection. From a US perspective, the most alarming out-of-area capabilities of the Russian navy remain its undersea forces, which likely have the capability to operate thousands of miles from home ports.

Not only have Russian forces changed greatly since the end of the Cold War, but so have a range of military technologies. Russia has expertly implemented and exploited advances that have occurred in the realms of undersea warfare, power projection, cyber warfare, and other modes of warfare. Russian submarines today are perhaps some of the most silent and deadly in the world. Russian missiles, launched from coastal-defence systems, long-range aircraft, and other delivery mechanisms, can now reach the capitals of almost all of Europe – not just those of the North Atlantic states. In addition, Russian hackers not only threaten our command-and-control systems, but also expertly and rapidly disseminate misleading propaganda across global information networks to support the Kremlin's goals. Finally, the Russian use of new modes of warfare and unconventional forces has required us to work diligently to develop new strategies to counter these methods. Overall, we must actively meet Russian challenges and, due to the growth of information technologies, the actions we do take could have much greater, and much more public, consequences than in previous decades.

The employment of such new capabilities by Russia is not necessarily, in itself, a cause for alarm. But Russia today uses these forces in ways that are clearly not only defensive. Almost everything that the Russian military has done in the recent past seems aimed at confronting and challenging NATO. For example, the recent construction of six new *Kilo*-class submarines with a greatly increased operational tempo is not a defensive undertaking. In September 2017, one of these improved *Kilo* attack submarines launched cruise missiles from the Eastern Mediterranean at targets in Syria.

Russian undersea actions are not random, but rather appear to be part of a newly and undeniably assertive strategy by the Kremlin. Russia's submarines are more active than ever across the entire North Atlantic, not only testing our reactions but also familiarising themselves with the environment in which we operate. Russia today has over 40 combat submarines, more than 20 of which are concentrated in the Northern Fleet. The potential for sudden and tragic events or accidents, combat operations, espionage, or some unforeseen new mode of warfare at sea cannot be ignored. As prudent operators and planners, we must understand and remain dominant in our undersea battlespace. It is not an exaggeration to claim that we are today engaged in a Fourth Battle of the Atlantic – one which we will win only by deterring conflict with our superior capabilities and advantages.

Russian improvements in undersea warfare are just one example of its desire to flex its muscles. To some, the 2016 highly publicised cruise of the *Kuznetsov* carrier represented another example of the Kremlin's desire for power projection, but the 33-year-old *Kuznetsov*, with only V/STOL-capable aircraft, does not come close to a modern US aircraft carrier. Nevertheless, Russia's concentration of forces in and around the Eastern Mediterranean, Crimea, Kaliningrad, and the High North can quickly and easily escalate into dangerous situations. Even minor incidents far from such high-profile deployments can rapidly spiral out of control. When a Russian Su-24 Fencer aircraft buzzed the USS *Donald Cook* in international waters in the Baltic Sea about 70 miles north of

Kaliningrad, it came within just 30 feet of the ship's superstructure. Not only is such behaviour the epitome of unsafe and unprofessional, but it could easily have resulted in miscalculation or a tragic escalation of an already dangerous situation. This type of activity by Russian aircraft is not uncommon in international airspace. They consistently test NATO's responses with their aggressive manoeuvres, which makes it all the more important for our commanders to be well trained and exercise the necessary restraint, while always being prepared to defend their forces.

How Does the Alliance Meet these Challenges?

Despite the urgency of the current situation in the North Atlantic, we are meeting these challenges as we always have: by maintaining superior joint, combined and multi-domain capabilities; by relying on the fundamental strengths of our Alliance as a partnership of forces; by demonstrating our common resolve; and by adopting new strategies and adaptations. These are, and always have been, the bedrock for NATO success.

The truth of the matter is that NATO forces, taken together, are significantly capable, postured, ready to deter and, if necessary, defeat any aggression we face. Our forces can respond to any of the challenges facing us, not only maritime but also cyber and unconventional. We are dominant in all domains – air, cyber, land and sea. Thus, despite its attempts at modernisation, the Russian military still has significant capability gaps when compared to US and NATO combined forces.

NATO derives its strength in the North Atlantic and beyond not only from our dominant capabilities but also from our true partnership of forces. The US Navy has recognised since the end of the Second World War that we will never 'go it alone'. We operate forward, across the globe, but always with our allies and partners. This is one of our fundamental strengths, and nowhere is this more evident than in the North Atlantic. Every day, the warships of NATO countries are at sea, maintaining control and security over this crucial water space and protecting international commerce and freedom of navigation there. Together, the undersea, surface, land and air assets of the most proximate NATO maritime states are capable, postured and ready to deter, and if needed, defeat aggression against the Alliance. And our forces are committed to standing ready, at all times, to operate in a unified manner, as true partners, whenever needed.

Nonetheless, such cooperation and commitment does not happen automatically, or in a vacuum. We must continually demonstrate our collective resolve and readiness against all challenges. Ever more frequently, NATO navies are utilised in critical counter-piracy, counterterrorism and migrant operations. These are missions that must not be abandoned or abjured, but we must also not allow ourselves to miss the long-term forest for the short-term trees. One day, Russian leadership may cease its aggressive and confrontational posture in the North Atlantic and rejoin the rules-based and peaceful European order. Until then, we in NATO must redouble our efforts to be partners, and not just allies, in the North Atlantic. We must invest strategically in ways that complement each other's forces and capabilities and avoid redundancy across our navies. Together, our combined navy partnership remains stronger than the sum of our individual navies.

Our partnerships and our demonstrations of resolve are ongoing and impressive, and the signals they send are unmistakable. We have the capabilities and will to ensure the independence, sovereignty and security of all NATO members. But, in this rapidly changing world, we must continue to adapt to keep our edge. We are strengthening our joint warfighting capabilities in ways that integrate all domain efforts across the entire battlespace. We are also adapting our strategies and ways of thinking to ensure our continued dominance in the North Atlantic and elsewhere. This is why NATO has re-evaluated the NATO Command Structure with a 360-degree approach that includes a new Joint Force Command to be focused on the North Atlantic.

In sum, these principles of superior multi-domain capabilities, partnership, resolve, and adaptation are the fundamental reasons why NATO is the most successful and greatest alliance in human history. By continuing to nurture the transatlantic relationships that we share, we can ensure a peaceful and prosperous Europe and North America for generations to come.

Next Steps

Despite our unity and strength, we still face a Russia that seems determined to operate outside internationally accepted norms and procedures. We do not seek a new Cold War, but rather a peaceful relationship. We continue to hold out the possibility that Russia will assume the role of a respected partner in the future. Thus, we will engage with Russia where our interests align. But we will also make it clear that the US and the entire NATO Alliance are ready and willing to defend every ally should the need arise. To maintain peace in Europe and the security of NATO, we will:

- Remain a strong and capable deterrent network of forces committed to regional security and regional stability.
- Maintain our unified and unshakeable commitment to Article 5.

- Demonstrate our commitment to self-determination, regional stability and collective defence of all of NATO.
- Maintain our technological edge and positive balance of forces today and into the future.
- Demonstrate, through our strategic communications and our actions, that we are a defensive Alliance committed to stability in Europe.
- Continue to operate, train and react to threats as a seamlessly connected partnership of forces that can, at will, interoperate where and when needed to meet any threats to our collective security, national sovereignty and the inviolability of the Articles of the Alliance.

Today, the most comprehensive and demonstrable manifestation of these principles in action is exercise *Trident Juncture*. The first *Trident Juncture* in 2015 mobilised over 36,000 air, land, maritime and special forces personnel from over 30 countries for activities in Spain, Portugal, Italy and the Mediterranean. At the time, it was the largest NATO live exercise since 2002 and demonstrated the ability of the NATO Response Force to work together seamlessly to conduct crisis response. In 2018, we will hold the exercise in Norway and expand it to involve more than 40,000 personnel from more than 30 NATO member and partner countries, including Norway's non-NATO neighbours Finland and Sweden. The exercise will focus on the challenge of operating in land, air and sea across the Northern region and against a highly capable adversary. As part of the scenario, the spearhead force of the Very High Readiness Joint Task Force (VJTF) will deploy within two to three days. *Trident Juncture* 2018 will be the largest NATO exercise in decades and show unmistakably that NATO is ready to defend and deter across the entire Alliance – from North America to Europe.

As an Alliance exercise, *Trident Juncture* is second to none in its message of unity, strength and readiness. We should thus endeavour to expand its scope and scale in the years to come. For example, we can and should train for distributed maritime operations, enabled by advanced communications, multi-sensor networks and coherent operating pictures. We should also look to actively exercise sea control to demonstrate and train our abilities to deny freedom of manoeuvre to any adversary. Critical to this is to increase our military-to-military engagement and other exercises within NATO. Further, we need to expand our exercises and operations further and further north – we must be able to show that any international water, however unforgiving, is not off limits to NATO forces and that we will defend the territory of Alliance members under Article 5.

Russian leadership will doubtless claim that such activities are escalatory. But *Trident Juncture* by itself is not aggressive and how Russia responds to it is up to Moscow. NATO forces will always train and operate in transparent and professional ways. If Russian forces act similarly (that is, with transparency), that is a sign of a healthy détente and we should encourage it as evidence that Russia can integrate into the peaceful and prosperous global order.

In the final analysis, the scale and breadth of *Trident Juncture* show clearly that NATO remains the most powerful and successful alliance of the twenty-first century. We can and will deploy substantial and highly capable combat forces to defend ourselves whenever and wherever needed. The exercise shows that we, as a solely defensive alliance, are irrevocably committed to Article 5 and the collective defence of all our member states together. Further, it shows that we possess a durable strategic advantage that no competitor can overcome. We are stronger together, and *Trident Juncture* is just one of many ways we demonstrate our strength.

CONCLUSION
DETERRENCE, DEFENCE AND DIALOGUE

JOHN ANDREAS OLSEN

Transatlantic Unity

NATO, the most successful military alliance in recent history, can only succeed if it appreciates and, to the extent possible, responds to the concerns of all its members. The principle of solidarity lies at the heart of NATO's founding treaty. As enshrined in Article 5 of the Washington Treaty, it remains the enduring principle that binds NATO's members together, committing them to protect and help each other. At the Brussels Summit in July 2018, all 29 members re-emphasised this unwavering responsibility: 'Any attack against one Ally will be regarded as an attack against us all'.[1] That principle of solidarity also requires each member to take primary responsibility for its own territorial integrity and the security of its immediate region; Article 3 states that allies 'will maintain and develop their individual and collective capacity to resist armed attack'. Article 3 underscores the principle of fair burden-sharing; investment in national defence is the basis for Article 5.

This Whitehall Paper has focused on NATO's northern region, arguing that Russia's military build-up constitutes the most important politico-military challenge to the defence of Europe today and in the foreseeable future. Russia's new order of battle – augmented by high commands optimised for short-notice readiness and prompt mobilisation – manifests itself in a theatre-scale warfare posture and an anti-access strategy that enables Russia to strike any location in Europe and project force far into the North Atlantic with precision and lethality. The authors of the chapters comprising this volume argue that Northern Europe can contain and counter Russia if the region stands together with its North American allies

---

[1] NATO, 'Brussels Summit Declaration', press release, 11 July 2018, paras 1, 33, <https://www.nato.int/cps/en/natohq/official_texts_156624.htm>, accessed 23 July 2018.

under the NATO umbrella; transatlantic unity is even more important now than it was during the Cold War.

Deterrence, Defence and Dialogue

Security in Northern Europe points to the renewed relevance of 'NATO in 3D': *deterrence*, *defence* and *dialogue*. This triad encompasses the Alliance's longstanding strategy, dating from NATO's inception in 1949, but must be recalibrated in view of Russia's current geostrategic posture. The challenge is to strengthen the first two elements to enable the third – something that NATO and its key partners can only achieve if they approach Russia from a position of strength. NATO must consider *deterrence* in the context of today's military-political realities, covering the full spectrum of nuclear, conventional, cyber and hybrid dimensions. The essence lies in political cohesion and unity backed by credible military force. *Defence* includes the ability to fight – jointly and combined – with updated contingency plans, a command-and-control apparatus fit for purpose, and an exercise and training regime that strengthens interoperability, readiness, responsiveness and sustainability. To ensure resilience, the armed forces of each NATO member must be connected both 'inwards' to its society at large – including total defence concepts that link defence sectors to other governmental and commercial elements – and 'outwards' to the forces of allies and trusted partners.

Deterrence and defence are linked intrinsically to *dialogue* and *détente*. This paper emphasises that NATO members must seek a constructive dialogue with Moscow through bilateral and multilateral engagements aimed at finding common ground for coexistence and partnership in line with a rules-based international order. To succeed, NATO members and partners must re-establish formal and informal contacts with Russian counterparts to improve understanding and avoid diplomatic provocation and military escalation, even if the parties subscribe to competitive strategies. Dialogue must start with a series of confidence-building measures such as agreements on arms control, mutual inspections and regimes for notification; that is, diplomatic measures that emphasise transparency and accountability. In the near term, this must begin with re-approaching Moscow with modest expectations to shape a climate of trust, stability and predictability without compromising Western liberal values.

Cash, Capabilities and Contributions

The means to empower 'NATO in 3D' is burden-sharing, with emphasis on three 'Cs': *cash*, *capabilities* and *contributions*. To ensure continued US leadership and commitment, European allies must increase their defence spending to the NATO target of 2 per cent of their respective GDPs by 2024, as agreed upon at the Wales Summit in 2014 and repeated at Warsaw in 2016 and Brussels in 2018. The 2 per cent allocation does not in itself ensure adequate capacities and capabilities, but to Washington it says a great deal about each ally's political commitment to the transatlantic Alliance. Moreover, more than 20 per cent of the increased defence budget must be invested in new weapon systems to ensure that each country has relevant high-end capabilities that underwrite credible deterrence and collective defence.

While the European allies must again focus on collective defence, they must also contribute to fighting terrorism and handling migration and human trafficking outside Europe. Such efforts, normally connected to a coalition of some sort, form part of NATO's larger burden-sharing scheme.

The combination of the 3Ds and the 3Cs defines both political commitment and military force. It constitutes a comprehensive approach to establishing a theatre-wide defence and security framework for Northern Europe – one that includes NATO's two key partners, Sweden and Finland. These two countries are about to achieve a high degree of interoperability with NATO; should a crisis occur in Northern Europe, there is every reason to believe that all the Nordic countries will engage in close cooperation with NATO to enable shared responses. The combination of the 3Ds and 3Cs also contributes to 'out-of-area' operations of various sorts, be it nation-building, security sector reforms or warfighting.

Security of the Wider North

This Whitehall Paper suggests that the Northern European countries are in an exceptionally good position to contribute to peace and stability. They have relatively stable democratic political systems in place and their economies are strong, at least compared to some other parts of Europe. Overall, they maintain positive relations and extensive cooperation. They also have a tradition of contributing to international coalitions, some having 'punched considerably above their weight' for a sustained period of time in Afghanistan and Iraq. Importantly, these countries have traditionally had a strong bond with North America and most have enhanced their defence agreements with the US bilaterally, trilaterally or multilaterally. European initiatives such as the Northern Group and the Joint Expeditionary Force (JEF), Nordic Defence Cooperation (NORDEFCO) and the Nordic-Baltic (NB 8) collaboration all strengthen both regional defence cooperation and the Alliance as a whole.

Thus, despite differing priorities and defence ambitions, the Northern Group countries exhibit a strong sense of solidarity and collective responsibility, as well as readiness to exploit opportunities for closer cooperation in the future. The five Nordic countries represent a political grouping with high standing and influence, and therefore a desirable partner in international affairs. However, the Northern Group also consists predominantly of 'small' countries; the UK and Germany undeniably have the greatest importance for defence and security in Northern Europe. The former is returning its attention to the North Atlantic and taking responsibility for ensuring freedom of the seas; the UK's new aircraft carriers can play a leading role in both Article 5 and expeditionary operations. Germany, for its part, is a key security provider in the broadest sense, as an economic powerhouse and a strong defender of multinational solutions. The most urgent priority for the German defence enterprise is to build up sufficient capabilities to counter Article 5 threats in Eastern Europe, but Germany also needs to take greater responsibility for the defence and security of the northern region. Viewing security through the prism of the Wider North – the Northern Group and North America combined – offers NATO and partners a theatre-wide approach that the contributors to this Whitehall Paper deem necessary for meeting the challenges of tomorrow.

Prospects

The main challenges Northern European countries face involve finding ways to make regional defence cooperation strategic rather than ad hoc, connect national strategies to NATO and US contingency plans with emphasis on timely reinforcements, overcome the regional Article 5 commitment gap represented by Sweden and Finland, and strengthen rather than erode the all-important NATO-EU partnership. The various authors argue that the Wider North must show unity of effort as it returns to 'hard' security issues. The partnership with the US still defines the Alliance; the US is the only country with the military power to deter, contain and counter Russia. Thus, the US must remain the 'benign hegemon' within the Alliance.

This Whitehall Paper emphasises the importance of connecting 'atlanticism' and 'continentalism'. These two outlooks must be seen as complementary and mutually reinforcing given today's multifaceted and complex security environment. In adopting this unifying perspective, NATO must balance responses to the air-land-centric challenge from the east with the air-maritime-oriented challenge from the north, and also improve its mastery of the cyber domain. NATO's new command structure represents a very positive step to ensure that the Alliance is 'fit for purpose', but NATO needs to invest more in high-end materiel and expand its regime of Article 5 exercises for its forces to become capable and sustainable on short notice.

The prerequisite for a stable and secure Northern Europe is an Alliance that combines national and regional efforts with a strong transatlantic relationship. The authors of this paper conclude that NATO members have taken significant steps to counter Russia's aggressive policies and actions, but that the Alliance and its partners need to do more. Given that the *end state* is a lasting peace in Europe with Russia as a partner in maintaining a rules-based international order, the *ways* consist of strengthening deterrence, defence and dialogue through the *means* of cash, capabilities and contributions. The *ends-ways-means* nexus offers a comprehensive approach to security based on the overarching imperative for each NATO member to support all the others when and where needed, but devote its primary attention to strengthening its own region.